Grand Tour
New Discoveries

Anthony Sellick

James Bury

Kaori Horiuchi

⌒ SEIBIDO

photographs by

iStockphoto
Imaginechina ／時事通信フォト
PSYKOTO / Carl Månsson / Kingkongphoto & www.celebrity-photos.com from Laurel Maryland, USA / Basile Morin / Lorenz Deconinck / Ian Kirk / kallerna / SELF Magazine / Advert: Medically approved Bile Beans. Wellcome Collection. In copyright. Source: Wellcome Collection. / Svetlana Grechkina / Jonn Leffmann / FDR Presidential Library & Museum / Template: Archivio Barillari's Story / Matias Tukiainen

---

音声ファイルのダウンロード／ストリーミング

CD マーク表示がある箇所は、音声を弊社 HP より無料でダウンロード／ストリーミングすることができます。下記 URL の書籍詳細ページに音声ダウンロードアイコンがございますのでそちらから自習用音声としてご活用ください。

https://www.seibido.co.jp/ad697

Grand Tour – New Discoveries

Copyright © 2024 by Anthony Sellick, James Bury, Kaori Horiuchi

PREFACE

During the 17th and 18th centuries wealthy young people took a trip around Europe in order to complete their education. They visited famous historical sites, learned languages, and made friends with people in various countries. The Grand Tour helped prepare them for life as international citizens.

The *Grand Tour* series of books looks at a variety of important trends that are shaping the modern world. Each book examines issues that affect our lives, which will change our lives in the future, and which *you* will influence in the future.

The topics covered in the essays range widely and are grouped into four sections: the worlds of culture and society, science and technology, business and economics, and politics and international relations. Included are topics that encourage you to look at an everyday thing from a new perspective, topics that showcase the amazing progress and discoveries that are being made, and topics which focus on aspects of the world that need to be changed or which are changing too slowly.

We hope that you will find these topics interesting and thought-provoking, and that they encourage you to learn more about them. We sincerely hope you enjoy *your* Grand Tour.

Anthony Sellick, James Bury, and Kaori Horiuchi

CONTENTS

Chapter 1

Who's the Fairest of Them All?

The Surprising Truth About Beauty

🌐 Topic Activation

Think about the topic of *beauty*. Write as many words connected to the topic as you can in the space below. Then, compare your words with a partner.

🌐 Useful Words

Choose a word from the list below to complete each sentence.

1. After spending a week in Okinawa they all had dark _____.

2. He had to go to hospital after a dog chased him and bit him on the _____.

3. Labradoodles are created by _____ Labrador dogs and poodles together.

4. She used her smartphone to cheat in the test, so she was _____.

5. It is common for people to feel some _____ before giving a speech.

| anxiety | butt | tans | breeding | disqualified |

🌐 Reading   1-02 ~ 08 🎧CD

02 🎧CD

1   In December 2021, 43 contestants taking part in a beauty contest in Saudi Arabia were disqualified because they had received treatments to make them more beautiful. The beauty contest was the King Abdulaziz Camel Festival, and all the contestants were camels. Does a beauty contest for camels seem surprising? Around
5 the world, there are beauty contests for dogs, cats, cows (in Vietnam), goats (in Lithuania), elephants (in Nepal), pigeons (in the US), and even tarantula spiders (in

the UK). What can this wide range of beauty contests tell us about human ideas of beauty?

03 CD

2 Scientific research indicates that beauty is a way for animals to show that they
10 are healthy and a good choice for breeding. In other words, the most beautiful individuals have the most offspring. However, the environmental conditions in different areas may result in different features being valued as being more beautiful, such as lighter-colored animals being preferred in snowy areas, and darker animals being preferred in rocky areas. Furthermore, not every animal can mate with the most
15 beautiful animal. Some will mate with the second most beautiful, some with the third most beautiful, and so on. These two facts mean that there will always be a lot of variety in beauty.

04 CD

3 In humans, this means that while our ideas of beauty are partly
20 biological, they are also partly cultural and partly individual. It also means that ideas of beauty will often be different in different places and at different times in history. When considering
25 beauty among cultures and historical periods we soon discover that there has never been a single idea of human beauty. For example, in ancient Greece, the people of Athens thought that
30 plump women with light skin were the most beautiful. But the people of the neighboring state of Sparta thought that muscular women with tans were the most beautiful.

05 CD

35 **4** Looking at pictures of famous fashion models or idols from 10 or 20 years ago, it is easy to see that beauty

In the 1950s, Marilyn Monroe, Audrey Hepburn, Ayako Wakao, and Pearl Bailey were famous for their beauty, but everything about them is different – except their beauty.

fashions can change very quickly. Why is this? Psychologists have discovered that just being famous can make you more beautiful. This is called the familiarity principle, and it means that the more often we see a person – and we see famous people a lot – the more beautiful we think they are. Consequently, as new people become famous and popular, our ideas of what is beautiful also change.

06 CD

5 Throughout history, artists like Leonardo da Vinci and Michelangelo have tried to show us the beauty that they see. But this may be very different from reality. Today we see this in the use of computer software to modify how people look, such as the photoshopping of models in magazines and the use of filters in online platforms like Instagram and TikTok. In other words, even the models in pictures look very different in real life. For example, in 2019, actor Jameela Jamil complained that a magazine had changed how her arms, knees, ankles, breasts, body shape, and skin color looked in a picture.

07 CD

6 The fact that advertisers, the media, and social media influencers do not show us how people really look is a big problem. It means that the products they sell or promote cannot make you look like the model in the advertisement, because that is not what the model really looks like. Furthermore, being exposed to such unnaturally beautiful images can make people feel dissatisfied with how they look. This is an especially important problem for teenagers who, because their bodies and faces are changing, often lack confidence in their appearance. Research in 2019 found that using Instagram made over 30 percent of teenage girls feel worse about their bodies. In addition, the more that people posted selfies online, the more dissatisfied they felt about their bodies, and the more they used filters to "fix" how they looked. Such feelings can be very damaging to our mental health and lead to increased anxiety, stress, depression, eating disorders, and even suicide.

08 CD

7 Ignoring reality and trying to be a fantasy version of ourselves is not healthy. Instead, we need to learn what nature has really taught us about beauty. The surprising truth about beauty is this: whether you are tall, short, thin, fat, have large breasts or small breasts, thin legs or thick legs, a small butt or a big butt, light skin or dark skin, light hair or dark hair, long hair or short hair, a flat stomach or a round stomach, big eyes or small eyes, thick eyebrows or thin eyebrows, body art or no body art, you are

beautiful. You are beautiful, and a lot more people think so than you realize. So, look
70 in the mirror and say hello to the beautiful person looking back at you.

Notes

the King Abdulaziz Camel Festival「アブデュルアジズ国王ラクダ・フェスティバル」ラクダの美を競うコンテストで，優勝者には多額の賞金が支払われる。 **Sparta**「スパルタ」古代ギリシャの都市国家。軍国主義的政治・教育体制で知られる。 **familiarity principle**「親しみの原理」社会心理学用語の「単純接触効果」と同じ意味で使われる。 **photoshop**「（画像処理ソフトで）写真を加工する」 **body art**「ボディアート」入れ墨，ピアス，整形手術などで身体を飾ること。

🌐 Questions for Understanding

Part 1 Look at the following statements about the passage. Write T if the statement is True, and F if it is False. Write the number of the paragraph where you find the answer in the parenthesis.

1) _____ In natural environments, lighter-colored animals have the most offspring.

[　　]

2) _____ People from different parts of ancient Greece had different ideas about beauty.

[　　]

3) _____ According to the passage, only beautiful people can become famous.

[　　]

4) _____ According to the passage, artists have always changed how people look.

[　　]

Part 2 Look at the following questions about the passage. Check the best answer for each.

1) What was surprising about the King Abdulaziz Camel Festival?

　　a. ☐ It included a beauty contest for goats.

　　b. ☐ It only featured lighter-colored animals.

　　c. ☐ A lot of contestants tried to cheat.

　　d. ☐ The most beautiful camels had the most offspring.

2) Which word has the closest meaning to the word "principle" in Paragraph 4?

a. ☐ dominant

b. ☐ rule

c. ☐ primary

d. ☐ assumption

3) According to the passage, why was Jameela Jamil unhappy?

a. ☐ Because Leonardo da Vinci's picture of her was very different from reality.

b. ☐ Because new people were more famous and popular than her.

c. ☐ Because TikTok filters did not make her look more beautiful.

d. ☐ Because a magazine picture of her had been photoshopped.

4) Which of the following statements about beauty are correct? (Choose all that apply)

a. ☐ Different cultures have different ideas of beauty.

b. ☐ Ideas of beauty can change in a short period of time.

c. ☐ Posting selfies online can help to improve our mental health.

d. ☐ Today, there is one idea of beauty that we all agree with.

Summary 1-09 CD

Fill each space with the best word from the list below.

offspring	confidence	modify	advertisers	exposed	mate

In nature, beauty is a way for animals that are ready to 1) _____ to show that they are healthy and can produce good quality 2) _____. In other words, beauty is a kind of advertising. Today, we are constantly 3) _____ to images of beautiful people in the media and online. However, the creators of these images often 4) _____ them so that what we see is not reality but a fantasy. This can cause people to lose 5) _____ in how they look which can damage their mental health. But the truth about beauty is not what 6) _____ want us to believe. The truth about beauty is that we are all beautiful to somebody.

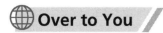 **Over to You**

Part 1 **Ask** Ask and answer the following questions.

1. Look at the picture on page 8. Who do you think is the most beautiful? Why?

2. Who is a famous person you think is beautiful?

3. Have you ever entered a beauty contest?

4. Have you ever posted a selfie online? If yes, did you use filters?

5. What part of someone's face do you think is the most beautiful?

Part 2 **Write** Choose ONE of the statements below. Prepare a short response giving your opinion.

> • The most beautiful thing about someone's face is their smile.
>
> • How you look is less important than how you behave.

_____

_____

_____

_____

Part 3 **Discuss** Look at the statement below. Do you agree or disagree? Why? Share your opinion with your classmates and find out what they think.

> Advertisers and social media influencers changing images to look more beautiful is no different from using makeup.

Chapter 2

Fan Fiction, Cosplay, and Rock Balancing

The World's Most Unusual Hobbies

🌐 Topic Activation

Think about the topic of *hobbies*. Write as many words connected to the topic as you can in the space below. Then, compare your words with a partner.

🌐 Useful Words

Choose a word from the list below to complete each sentence.

1. I started working here six months ago, so I am _____ new here.

2. Don't worry, mom! It's not a permanent tattoo. It's only _____.

3. Have you seen *Super Sentai IV*? It's the _____ to *Super Sentai III*.

4. I really _____ all of your help, so please accept this thank you gift.

5. If you have some _____, I can fix the broken chair right now.

temporary	appreciate	relatively	sequel	glue

🌐 Reading   1-10 ~ 15 CD

10 CD

1　What do you like to do in your free time? Maybe you like to watch movies, surf the internet, play games, or hang out with your friends. These are all popular activities that many people enjoy. However, while you may spend a lot of your free time doing them, they are not hobbies. So, what is a hobby and how is it different from a pastime?

5　A pastime is a free-time activity that we enjoy doing, such as listening to music. A hobby is a free-time activity that we are passionate about doing. For example, while

13

anyone can listen to music anytime, learning to play a musical instrument requires practice and dedication. This means that everyone has pastimes, but not everyone has hobbies. Popular hobbies around the world include gardening, team sports, cooking, fishing, martial arts, bird watching, and yoga. In fact, almost any activity, from astronomy to zumba, is someone's hobby. Let's look at some of the more unusual hobbies people have.

11 CD

2 *Writing:* Reading is one of the most popular pastimes. However, some readers are not satisfied with only reading their favorite stories, they are also inspired to write new ones. This is called fan fiction. While fans have been writing unofficial stories about their favorite characters since at least the 17th century, when Alonso Fernández de Avellaneda wrote his own sequel to Cervantes' popular novel *Don Quixote*, modern fan fiction began in the 1960s. Fans of the science fiction series *Star Trek* in the US began writing and sharing their own stories about the show and, at the same time, manga fans in Japan began writing their own manga, called *dōjinshi*. The development of the world wide web in the 1990s made it easy to write, share, read, and review fan fiction, and the hobby rapidly gained popularity. Today, fan fiction writers have their own conventions, such as Japan's Comiket, which began in 1975, some have become professional writers, and some fan fiction has been made into movies.

12 CD

3 *Costuming:* Like fan fiction, cosplay has a longer history than many people realize. Dressing up as fictional characters for themed parties has been a popular pastime since the 15th century in Europe and the 17th century in China. However, perhaps the first modern cosplay happened at the 1st World Science Fiction Convention in New York in 1939. As

Cosplayers in France, 2022

cosplay became more popular in the US, it also spread around the world, reaching the UK in 1953 and Japan in 1978. The Japanese style of cosplay has been so influential that many people think the hobby began in Japan. In fact, the word *cosplay* was created by Japanese reporter Nobuyuki Takahashi in 1984 after he saw cosplayers at a science fiction convention in Los Angeles.

13 CD

40 **4** *Balancing:* A hobby that gained popularity in the 2010s is rock balancing, which is the art of arranging stones in seemingly impossible ways without using any tools or glue. After creating a piece of
45 rock art, most rock balancers photograph their creations and then knock the rocks over. This means that rock balancing is a form of temporary art, that is, it is an art form which is intended to be experienced
50 for only a short time, like dance. Even

Rock balancing creates seemingly impossible towers of rocks

though it is a relatively new hobby, there are already rock balancing contests, such as the Balanced Art World International Festival in Canada, and the European Stone-Stacking Championships in Scotland.

14 CD

5 Most human activities have both good and bad aspects, and the same is true of
55 our hobbies. While many writers appreciate fan fiction, some do not, and have sued fan fiction writers for stealing their ideas. Many cosplay enthusiasts have experienced sexual harassment, and bullying among cosplayers is not uncommon. Finally, because rock balancers move rocks around, practicing the hobby in natural locations can cause damage to the local environment and can even kill small animals. In fact, because of
60 the potential damage to the environment, in many US national parks moving rocks is a crime.

15 CD

6 Hobbies can take up a lot of our time and can be expensive. In addition, it is possible for a passion to become an obsession. When an activity changes from being something we want to do into something we have to do, it stops being fun and can be
65 bad for our mental health. However, for most people having a hobby is beneficial. Hobbies can make us feel happier, more satisfied with our lives and our jobs, and can also improve our health by reducing stress. So, what are *you* passionate about doing?

martial arts「武道」柔道，空手，剣道，カンフーなどスポーツとして行われるもの。　**Cervantes**「セルバンテス（1547-1616）」Miguel de Cervantes Saavedra　スペインの小説家・劇作家。代表作『ドン・キホーテ』（1605-15）は主人公ドン・キホーテと従者サンチョ・パンサが騎士道修行の旅に出る諷刺小説。ミュージカル『ラ・マンチャの男』の原作。　**Star Trek**「スター・トレック」米国の SF テレビドラマシリーズ。1966 年に放映されて以来テレビアニメや映画，ドラマの新シリーズが制作され，熱狂的なファンが多い。

Questions for Understanding

Part 1 Look at the following statements about the passage. Write T if the statement is True, and F if it is False. Write the number of the paragraph where you find the answer in the parenthesis.

1) _____ A hobby is a free-time activity that we enjoy doing, such as watching movies. [   ]

2) _____ *Dōjinshi* is a kind of fan fiction which was first written in the 1960s. [   ]

3) _____ Many people believe that cosplay originated in Japan. [   ]

4) _____ Rock balancers can compete in international competitions. [   ]

Part 2 Look at the following questions about the passage. Check the best answer for each.

1) According to the passage, what is fan fiction?

    a. ☐ Stories written by science fiction fans

    b. ☐ A story published on the internet

    c. ☐ An unofficial story written by a fan

    d. ☐ A sequel to an original story

2) Which of the following statements about cosplay is correct?

    a. ☐ Cosplay began in China during the 15th century.

    b. ☐ Japanese people began cosplaying almost 40 years after British people.

    c. ☐ The first modern cosplay was at a convention for science fiction fans in New York.

    d. ☐ Noboyuki Takahashi was a famous cosplayer in Los Angeles during the 1980s.

3) Which word has the closest meaning to the word "influential" in Paragraph 3?

    a. ☐ impotent

    b. ☐ controlling

    c. ☐ unimportant

    d. ☐ significant

4) Which of the following statements about hobbies are correct? (Choose all that apply)

    a. ☐ Being passionate about a free-time activity can sometimes lead to bullying.

    b. ☐ Being passionate about a free-time activity can help to reduce stress.

    c. ☐ After a while, hobbies stop being fun and are bad for our mental health.

    d. ☐ Most people are happier if they do not have any hobbies.

🌐 Summary 1-16 💿

Fill each space with the best word or phrase from the list below.

dedication	hang out	enthusiasts	obsessions	beneficial	conventions

Spending time doing a hobby can have **1)** _____ effects on our lives. Hobbies can help reduce stress and provide a fun reason to **2)** _____ with our friends. **3)** _____ of hobbies like fan fiction and cosplay even attend **4)** _____ with thousands of other people who share their passion and **5)** _____ . However, we must be careful that the hobbies we enjoy do not make us treat other people badly or become **6)** _____ that control us.

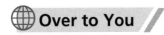 **Over to You**

Part 1 Ask and answer the following questions.

1. What do you like to do in your free time?

2. How often do you do it?

3. How much time do you spend doing it?

4. Is it a good way of making new friends?

5. Do you think you will continue to do it in the future?

Part 2 Choose ONE of the statements below. Prepare a short response giving your opinion.

- People spend too much money on their hobbies and pastimes.
- Hobbies can help us to achieve our dreams.

_____

_____

_____

_____

Part 3 Look at the statement below. Do you agree or disagree? Why? Share your opinion with your classmates and find out what they think.

Hobbies that you do with other people are better than hobbies that you do alone.

Chapter 3

It's All a Part of the Game

The Ethics of Sport

🌐 Topic Activation

Think about the topic of *sport*. Write as many words connected to the topic as you can in the space below. Then, compare your words with a partner.

🌐 Useful Words

Choose a word from the list below to complete each sentence.

1. My hometown has a famous _____ festival.

2. Even in a tough competition it is important to respect your _____.

3. The motorist was _____ for using his phone while driving.

4. The size of the audience had a big _____ on the players.

5. Toyota and Nintendo have strong global _____.

effect	annual	fined	opponent	reputations

🌐 Reading   1-17 ~ 23 🎵CD

17 🎵CD

1   One of the most popular running races in China is the annual Shenzhen Half Marathon. It is hosted in China's fourth largest city and it typically attracts about 16,000 runners. However, despite its popularity, in November 2018, the race faced controversy when 258 runners were caught cheating. Police traffic cameras showed
5 237 participants taking short cuts through bushes, cutting approximately three kilometers off the full 21-kilometer distance. Organizers also discovered 18 runners

wearing fake bibs and three people who competed under false names. News of the cheating led one of China's biggest newspaper publications, *The People's Daily*, to urge citizens to "respect sporting spirit" in an editorial. While this example is from an
10 amateur race, cheating in sports happens at all levels and takes many forms. Let's look at some of the most common ways of cheating and some of the most famous examples of them.

18 CD

2 *Performance enhancing drugs (PEDs):* One of the most common ways of
15 gaining an unfair advantage over rivals is by taking banned substances that can improve performance, such as steroids. This is known as "doping." These drugs can enable an athlete to train harder for
20 longer, can increase concentration, and can help muscles to recover more quickly. There have been many high-profile

Taking PEDs can enhance athletic performance

individuals that have been caught taking PEDs, such as Lance Armstrong (cycling — 2012), Maria Sharapova (tennis — 2016), and Kamila Valieva (ice skating — 2022).
25 However, the scandal of doping happens on a larger scale, too. In 2016, Russian athletes were banned from competing in a wide range of sports, including the Olympics, following the discovery of a systematic state-sponsored program of using PEDs.

19 CD

3 *Simulation:* Another common way of cheating is tricking a referee or official, for example by claiming that an opponent has committed a foul or other illegal action,
30 or by pretending to be injured to get an opponent punished. This is particularly common in soccer matches where players "dive" in order to gain a free kick or get a player from the other team sent off. In the 2002 Soccer World Cup held in South Korea and Japan, Brazil's Rivaldo faked a head injury after a ball had been kicked at him by a player from Turkey even though the ball had really hit his leg. The Turkish
35 player was sent off and Brazil won the match. A more gruesome example happened during a rugby match in England in 2009 when a player bit a capsule containing fake blood. This made the referee believe he was bleeding and allowed him to be substituted.

20 CD

4 *Equipment:* As the equipment used in sports can greatly affect performance, many cheats try to find a way to manipulate some of the tools they use to gain an advantage. In 2015, the New England Patriots American football team was fined $1 million and lost some future draft picks after it was found that team members had under-inflated some of the balls used in the AFC Championship game. They did this to make it easier for their players to grip the balls.

21 CD

5 *Physical attack:* One of the most unethical and brutal examples of cheating in sports history occurred in one of the most graceful sports. Tonya Harding and Nancy Kerrigan were rival ice skaters who both wanted to win the 1994 US Figure Skating Championships. However, just before the competition, a man attacked Kerrigan with a metal pole and broke her leg. As a result, she could not take part in the competition. It was found that Harding, her husband, and her bodyguard had hired the man who broke Kerrigan's leg.

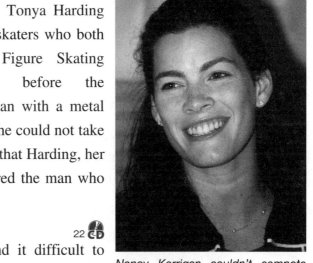

Nancy Kerrigan couldn't compete after being attacked

22 CD

6 *Why cheat?* Many people find it difficult to understand why some athletes cheat, but there are many reasons. These include getting medals, social recognition, prize money, bragging rights, and even to get a result that allows them to enter a higher-level competition, such as an Ironman Triathlon or the Boston Marathon.

23 CD

7 *Why does it matter?* Cheating is a major issue as it devalues the efforts of those who compete honestly. In the case of professional sport, it impacts on peoples' earnings, contracts, and reputations. It also affects the way that cheating is viewed by the watching audience. If a professional cheats and is not punished, or if they are successful as a result, that behavior could encourage others to cheat in everyday life. That is something we definitely do not want.

🌐 Questions for Understanding

Part 1 Look at the following statements about the passage. Write T if the statement is True, and F if it is False. Write the number of the paragraph where you find the answer in the parenthesis.

1) _____ In 2018, 258 participants of the Shenzhen Half Marathon were caught taking short cuts. [   ]

2) _____ In 2009, a rugby player in England bit a capsule containing fake blood after being substituted. [   ]

3) _____ The New England Patriots American football team under-inflated balls so that they would be easier to grip. [   ]

4) _____ Tonya Harding and Nancy Kerrigan competed at the 1994 US Figure Skating Championships. [   ]

Part 2 Look at the following questions about the passage. Check the best answer for each.

1. Which word has the closest meaning to the word "controversy" in Paragraph 1?

   a. ☐ danger

   b. ☐ excitement

   c. ☐ fascination

   d. ☐ trouble

2. What can PEDs **not** do?

    a. ☐ Help an athlete train harder for longer

    b. ☐ Help an athlete concentrate better

    c. ☐ Help muscles recover more quickly

    d. ☐ Help individuals catch people "doping"

3. What is a "dive" an example of?

    a. ☐ A way of tricking a referee or official

    b. ☐ A match at the 2002 Soccer World Cup

    c. ☐ A head injury

    d. ☐ A ball that has been kicked at another player

4. What could encourage people to cheat in everyday life?

    a. ☐ The efforts of those who compete honestly

    b. ☐ Professional sports players' earnings, contracts, and reputations

    c. ☐ The views of the audience watching sport

    d. ☐ Professional cheating and not being punished

⊕ Summary   1-24 💿

Fill each space with the best word from the list below.

manipulate	rivals	role	substances	urge	unethical

Sports play an important **1)** _____ in many peoples' lives. When people take sports seriously, they can feel a(n) **2)** _____ to try and find an advantage over their **3)** _____ . This can lead to cheating in order to **4)** _____ results. This can be done in various ways, including taking prohibited **5)** _____ and "diving." However, despite the reasons cheats give for their actions, it is important to note that if cheating in sports goes unpunished, it could encourage **6)** _____ behavior in everyday life.

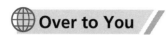 **Over to You**

Part 1 Ask and answer the following questions.

1. Do you play any sports?

2. Do you like to watch sports on TV?

3. Who is your favorite sportsperson or athlete?

4. Have you ever cheated in a sports game or on a test?

5. What do you think of athletes that take PEDs?

Part 2 Choose ONE of the statements below. Prepare a short response giving your opinion.

- Sports players and athletes are good role models.
- Sports cheats should receive lifetime bans.

_____

_____

_____

_____

Part 3 Look at the statement below. Do you agree or disagree? Why? Share your opinion with your classmates and find out what they think.

Using PEDs should not be prohibited.

Chapter 4

I'm Bored

How Boredom Can Be Good for Us

🌐 **Topic Activation**

Think about the topic of *boredom*. Write as many words connected to the topic as you can in the space below. Then, compare your words with a partner.

🌐 **Useful Words**

Choose a word from the list below to complete each sentence.

1. The passenger next to me on the flight was very _____. He wouldn't stop moving.

2. Many people find bungee jumping a very _____ experience.

3. The achievements of Olympic athletes are _____ for most people.

4. Meditation is one way that we can try to _____ our feelings.

5. Inventors and designers are often practical and _____ people.

| curious | intense | regulate | restless | unattainable |

🌐 **Reading**   1-25 ~ 30 🎧

25 🎧

1   Would you enjoy sitting alone in an empty room for 15 minutes with nothing to do? Most people would not enjoy this experience. In fact, one study showed that 67 percent of men and 25 percent of women preferred to give themselves electric shocks rather than sit quietly in an empty room. Boredom is generally viewed as an
5 unpleasant feeling, but is being bored actually a bad thing?

2 Many people feel dissatisfied, restless, and uncomfortable when they are bored. This makes them look for distractions, such as using social media,
10 playing video games, or watching movies. However, such activities are short-term solutions which, like an addiction, can lead to more intense stimulation being needed

What are the benefits of being bored?

to avoid boredom in the future. This is why boredom is often associated with fast-
15 developing self-control problems, including drug abuse, gambling, and binge-eating. However, while the negative aspects of being bored are well-known, there are also some benefits to experiencing boredom which are often overlooked. These include improving our mental health, our creativity, and our desire to try new things.

3 At a time when there is so much information readily available, especially on our
20 phones, we can feel overloaded and this can cause stress. Also, scrolling through social media can make us more competitive and feel like our lives are not as good as the unattainable, perfect lives that everyone in our social media feeds seems to have. This habit is sometimes called "doomscrolling," and it can leave us feeling frustrated, depressed, and even angry. However, taking a break from social media long enough to
25 feel bored can be a valuable opportunity to reduce these negative feelings. Experiencing boredom can reduce the negative effects of social media by helping us build tolerance of less-than-perfect situations. This increased tolerance is correlated with the development of self-control skills and allows us to manage our frustrations and regulate our emotions better. This is especially important for children, so
30 experiencing boredom can help them to develop valuable skills they will need later in life.

4 It has also been found that boredom can increase creativity and problem-solving skills by encouraging people to actively think and reflect. In one study, when people were made to do boring tasks they used their imagination more and thought in a
35 variety of different ways. This shows that boredom and the absence of external stimulation can lead to creative ways of thinking and the discovery of new ideas.

According to neuroscientist Alicia Walf, ideas that we may have had in our minds for a long time can be focused on when we are bored. Consequently, they become better developed. Many inventors, artists, and thought-leaders, including Archimedes, 40 Picasso, and Steve Jobs, claimed that their most creative ideas came to them when they were bored or doing unexciting things like gardening or having a bath.

29

5 Boredom can also motivate people to try and find new and exciting things to do. It is the feeling of boredom and 45 dissatisfaction that makes humans curious and willing to challenge established ideas and practices. Being bored also encourages us to change our goals and projects to others that are more fulfilling than the ones 50 we are currently pursuing. On a societal

People often try new things when they are bored

level, this can lead to great achievements and advances. On a personal level, it can help us get to know ourselves better.

30

6 Given these benefits, perhaps we should embrace boredom. In Italy this is called "*il dolce far niente*," translated as "the sweetness of doing nothing." Author James 55 Clear writes that we should try to "fall in love with boredom." But many people are finding this increasingly difficult to do, especially when work, chores, and other tasks are becoming more time-consuming in our modern lives. It is also important to acknowledge that just being bored will not positively impact on our lives. Rather, it is how we react to the boredom that is most important. If we can approach boredom in a 60 proactive way and view it as an opportunity to do something beneficial that will help us in some way, we could all see an increase in our mental strength, creativity, and motivation to expand our horizons. So, next time you feel bored, do not reach for your phone, but instead ask yourself, "How can I use this as an opportunity to better myself?"

binge-eating「過食」 **feed**「フィード」インスタグラムなどのソーシャルメディアのホーム画面。配信の流れや更新を表示する場所のこと。 **doomscrolling**「ドゥームスクローリング」doom は「(悪い) 運命」を意味する語で，ネット上でネガティブな情報ばかりを検索し続けること。 **neuroscientist**「神経科学者」 **Archimedes**「アルキメデス (287?-212b.c.)」ギリシャの数学者・科学者。

🌐 Questions for Understanding

Part 1 | Look at the following statements about the passage. Write T if the statement is True, and F if it is False. Write the number of the paragraph where you find the answer in the parenthesis.

1) _____ Boredom is commonly linked to fast-developing self-control problems.

[   ]

2) _____ Many successful people have their most creative ideas when they are bored or doing unexciting things. [   ]

3) _____ Boredom encourages people to follow established ideas and practices.

[   ]

4) _____ Recently, work, chores, and other tasks are taking less time to complete.

[   ]

Part 2 | Look at the following questions about the passage. Check the best answer for each.

1. What do a lot of people in social media feeds seem to have?

   a. ☐ Feelings of being overloaded and stressed

   b. ☐ Lives that are perfect and unattainable

   c. ☐ Feelings of frustration, depression, and anger

   d. ☐ A tolerance of less-than-perfect situations

2. Which word has the closest meaning to the word "correlated" in Paragraph 3?

a. ☐ controlled

b. ☐ designed

c. ☐ linked

d. ☐ mirrored

3. According to Alicia Walf, what can be focused on when we are bored?

a. ☐ Our creativity and problem-solving skills

b. ☐ External stimulation and creative ways of thinking

c. ☐ Ideas we may have had in our minds for a long time

d. ☐ Unexciting things like gardening or having a bath

4. Which of the following statements about boredom are correct? (Choose all that apply)

a. ☐ Boredom makes people look for distractions.

b. ☐ Boredom can lead to the discovery of new ideas.

c. ☐ Boredom encourages people to continue pursuing their current goals.

d. ☐ The way that people respond to boredom is very important.

Summary   1-31

Fill each space with the best word from the list below.

> achievements   motivate   overloaded   proactive   reflect   stimulation

When people are bored they often feel dissatisfied and uncomfortable. This makes them look for external 1) _____, such as using their smartphones. However, as there is so much information available to us, when we do that, we can feel 2) _____ and stressed. One way to avoid this is to use our free time to actively think and 3) _____ on our thoughts and feelings. Using boredom in this way can 4) _____ people to find new and exciting things to do. It can also lead to great 5) _____ and advances on a societal level. But, to gain these benefits, boredom must be approached in a 6) _____ way.

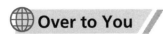 **Over to You**

Part 1 Ask and answer the following questions.

1. Do you often feel bored?

2. What do you do when you are waiting for something?

3. When was the last time you felt very bored?

4. How do you feel when you have nothing to do?

5. Which school subject did you find most boring?

Part 2 Choose ONE of the statements below. Prepare a short response giving your opinion.

- Boredom generally leads to negative outcomes.
- It is important to learn how to control boredom.

_____

_____

_____

_____

Part 3 Look at the statement below. Do you agree or disagree? Why? Share your opinion with your classmates and find out what they think.

Children should not always have busy schedules.

Chapter 5

Go Whistle!

A Different Way of Communicating

🌐 Topic Activation

Think about the topic of *communication*. Write as many words connected to the topic as you can in the space below. Then, compare your words with a partner.

🌐 Useful Words

Choose a word from the list below to complete each sentence.

1. When writing an essay it is important to _____ linking phrases effectively.

2. The man threw his cards on the table to _____ his anger at losing the game.

3. Many famous actors _____ in the new movie.

4. Children learn languages by _____ people around them.

5. The _____ of the island are proud of their unique culture.

| demonstrate | feature | incorporate | inhabitants | mimicking |

🌐 Reading   1-32 ~ 38 🎵CD

32 🎵CD

1 If you take a moment to think about how many different languages there are in the world, you will realize humans have an amazing linguistic diversity. Some languages, like Thai and Vietnamese, use tones. Some languages, like the Khoisan languages of southern Africa, incorporate clicks into words, using them as
5 independent syllables. But can you imagine a language that does not use conventional

words at all?

2 In many places around the world whistles are used in a range of ways. A whistle can be used to express a feeling of surprise, to gain someone's attention, and to signal annoyance or frustration (often at sporting events). Whistles can also be used to give instructions, such as police officers using whistles to control traffic or shepherds using whistles to instruct their dogs. However, according to Professor Julien Meyer, communication using whistles can be as flexible and versatile as normal speech.

3 In fact, Meyer's research with collaborators all over the world identifies over 70 languages that consist solely of whistles, including Mazatec in Mexico, Wayãpi in Amazonia, Banen in Africa, Akha in Southeast Asia, and Béarnese in the Pyrenees mountains between France and Spain. This is not a new phenomenon, and a number of sources reveal that whistled languages are an ancient tradition

Whistled languages are used all over the world, including Amazonia

found all over the globe. They were described in the fifth century BCE by Greek historian Herodotus and they also feature in several Chinese texts from the second to eighth centuries CE, including the eighth century *Treatise of Whistling*, or *Xiaozhi*, which is one of the earliest known works on phonetics.

4 Whistled languages serve a lot of different purposes and have a lot of potential benefits. One of these is communicating over long distances quickly. Whistles can travel much further than normal speech and in open spaces they can reach as far as 8km. This is particularly useful for farmers in mountainous regions who need to pass messages to each other. Whistles are also very useful in forest areas as they can penetrate the trees and foliage more easily than normal words or sounds. When combined with the fact that they tend to scare animals less than other sounds, whistles can be a very effective way for hunters to communicate.

5 For many people it is difficult to imagine how whistles can be used to convey

important information, but that is also one of the strengths of whistled languages. As they are difficult for outsiders to understand, whistled languages can be used as a way of transmitting secret or sensitive messages. This is especially useful in times of war. For example, during the Second World War, the Australian army recruited people
40 from Papua New Guinea to whistle messages over the radio so that they could not be understood by the enemy. It is also useful in times of love. Compared with spoken conversations, it is hard to identify peoples' individual "voices" from their whistles and that makes it the perfect language for shy young couples to communicate secretly, as demonstrated in many Hmong communities.

37 CD

45 **6** Despite the benefits of using whistled languages, and many interesting findings associated with them, such as blackbirds learning and mimicking Silbo Gomero, a whistled language used on one of the Canary Islands, many are in danger of dying out.
50 The whistled language called Sfyria, which is used on the Greek island of Evia, is one of the rarest and most endangered languages in the world. For the last two thousand years, the island's inhabitants have passed down the language to their children. But in the last

Blackbirds have been found mimicking whistled human languages

55 few decades, due to the population decreasing and many older residents no longer being able to make the whistle sounds as they lose their teeth, there are now only six people left on the planet who can still "speak" this unspoken language.

38 CD

7 Whistled speech is a fascinating area of linguistics which can lead to a better
60 understanding of the cultures that use it and language development in general. Linguistic research has shown that we are all able to learn whistled languages so, to protect these threatened languages, we should all give whistling a try!

Khoisan「コイサン語族」南部アフリカのコイ人とサン人の総称。単音節の語幹，吸着音（舌打ちと同じ種類の破裂音）を言語の特徴とする。　**versatile**「汎用性のある，多目的な」　**Mazatec**「マサテック（族の言語）」　**Wayãpi**「ワイアピ」Wayampi とも表記される。　**Amazonia**「アマゾニア」南米のアマゾン川流域。　**Banen**「バネン」　**Akha**「アカ（族の言語）」　**Béarnese**「ベアルネーゼ」　**BCE**「紀元前」Before the Common Era の略。非キリスト教徒が B.C. の代わりに用いる表記。　**Herodotus**「ヘロドトス（484?-425?B.C.）」ギリシャの歴史家。歴史の父と言われる人物。　**CE**「西暦」Common Era＝Christian Era キリスト教徒以外にも受け入れられる表現として使われる。　**treatise**「（学術）論文，専門書」Treatise of Whistling は中国の道教に影響を受けた口笛の技法についての専門書。Xiaozhi も同じく口笛についての論文。　**phonetic**「（漢字の）表音要素」　**foliage**「（1本または複数の木全体の）葉，群葉」　**Hmong**「モン族」フモンあるいはモングと表記することもある。　**Silbo Gomero**「シルボ・ゴメーロ」　**Sfyria**「スフィリア」　**Evia**「エヴィア」ギリシャの東方にある島。

🌐 Questions for Understanding

Part 1 Look at the following statements about the passage. Write T if the statement is True, and F if it is False. Write the number of the paragraph where you find the answer in the parenthesis.

1) _____ According to Julien Meyer whistled languages are not as flexible or versatile as normal speech. [   ]

2) _____ Whistled languages can be found all over the globe. [   ]

3) _____ Australian soldiers whistled messages over the radio in the Second World War. [   ]

4) _____ It is not possible for everyone to learn a whistled language. [   ]

Part 2 Look at the following questions about the passage. Check the best answer for each.

1. What do Khoisan languages **not** include?

   a. ☐ tones

   b. ☐ clicks

   c. ☐ independent syllables

   d. ☐ conventional words

2. Which word has the closest meaning to the word "conventional" in Paragraph 1?

    a. ☐ ancient

    b. ☐ interesting

    c. ☐ traditional

    d. ☐ unusual

3. Which of the following statements are reasons why whistled language are useful for farmers? (Choose all that apply)

    a. ☐ Whistles can be used to communicate over long distances.

    b. ☐ Whistles can travel farther than normal speech.

    c. ☐ Whistles can penetrate trees and foliage easily.

    d. ☐ Whistles are difficult for outsiders to understand.

4. What is a problem for many whistled languages?

    a. ☐ They have many associated interesting findings.

    b. ☐ They are in danger of dying out.

    c. ☐ They get passed down from parents to children.

    d. ☐ They make older people lose their teeth.

🌐 Summary
1-39 🎧

Fill each space with the best word from the list below.

annoyance	fascinating	linguistic	phenomenon	solely	threat

There are many different languages in the world and humans have great 1) _____ diversity. While many people use whistles to signal 2) _____ and other emotions, some languages are made up 3) _____ of whistles. This 4) _____ is not new and there are many examples of whistled languages around the globe. However, even though researchers find these languages 5) _____, many are now under 6) _____ of extinction. This is a shame as they can help us understand other cultures and language development in general.

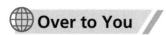 **Over to You**

Part 1 **Ask and answer the following questions.**

1. Can you whistle?

2. How many languages can you speak?

3. If you could learn any language, what would it be?

4. Have you ever tried to teach a language?

5. What do you think are important phrases to know when traveling?

Part 2 **Choose ONE of the statements below. Prepare a short response giving your opinion.**

- We should learn some phrases of the local language before traveling abroad.

- It is important to protect dying languages.

_____

_____

_____

_____

Part 3 **Look at the statement below. Do you agree or disagree? Why? Share your opinion with your classmates and find out what they think.**

Schools should not teach a foreign language
until students are proficient in their own language.

Chapter 6

Now You See It

What Magic Can Tell Us About Our Minds

🌐 Topic Activation

Think about the topic of *magic*. Write as many words connected to the topic as you can in the space below. Then, compare your words with a partner.

🌐 Useful Words

Choose a word from the list below to complete each sentence.

1. I am colorblind. I cannot _____ any difference between red and green.

2. He says he loves her, but he is _____ her. All he wants is her money.

3. I don't know how my boss does it. It's obvious that he's _____ me, but I just can't say no when he asks me to work late.

4. I was a(n) _____ in the Tokyo Marathon. I didn't run, though. I was a member of the support staff.

5. It can be difficult to _____ old electrical appliances.

manipulating	discard	participant	exploiting	perceive

🌐 Reading 1-40 ~ 45 🎧

40 🎧

1 Have you ever been amazed by a magic trick? Did you try, and fail, to work out what happened? You are not alone. Magicians have been fooling their audiences for a very long time. The oldest known magic trick, using a specially designed water bowl, was being performed in Greece over 2,500 years ago, and may have originated in

37

India almost 5,000 years ago. The same trick was also being used by the Chimu people of Peru at least 700 years ago. Another trick, using cups and balls, was described by the Roman writer Seneca in 65 CE. Amazingly, magicians are still performing both tricks today.

41 CD

2 The fact that some magic tricks have been performed for thousands of years and discovered independently by different cultures indicates that magicians are exploiting universal features of the human mind. Consequently, scientists have begun investigating magic tricks to gain a better understanding of how our minds work. So, what can magic tricks teach us about ourselves?

42 CD

3 During the performance of a trick, magicians often use various techniques to change the way we perceive, remember, or think about what we are experiencing. This is known as misdirection. For example, a magician may throw a ball into the air once, and then again, and then a third time, but the ball vanishes on the third toss. How is this possible? The trick works because of the way we perceive events occurring around us. Although it feels like we see everything that is happening, in reality our brains only focus on a small number of important things. Furthermore, in order to decide what is important, our brains try to predict what will happen next. Finally, humans are social animals, so the actions and behaviors of other people are very important. This means that we spend more time looking at the magician's face than we realize. The result of this is that while the magician throws the ball twice, and then only pretends to throw it the third time, nearly 70 percent of the audience will report that they saw the ball move up into the air and disappear.

Magic tricks and illusions can reveal how we think …

43 CD

4 Another way that magicians can fool us is by manipulating how we make a

38

choice. For example, if a magician deals four cards in front of you and asks you to choose one card, they know that around 60 percent of people will choose the card that is directly in front of them. Another way that magicians do this is by offering people a choice that is not really a choice. Look at the two conversations below. Did the
40 participant really have a choice?

Magician:	First, we need to decide if we will use the red card or the green card. Please pick one.	Magician:	First, we need to decide if we will use the red card or the green card. Please pick one.
Participant:	Green.	Participant:	Red.
Magician:	Green? Okay, I will discard the red card. Now, please read the green card.	Magician:	Red? Okay, I will discard the red card. Now, please read the green card.

It is not just magicians that use this kind of manipulation, of course. The reason that many supermarkets offer their customers free, but small, samples of tasty food is because eating a little food makes you hungrier, and hungry people buy more food.

44 CD

5   The scientific study of magic tricks can tell us a
45 lot about how we experience the world. However, some scientists have started using magic tricks to help them understand how animals perceive the world, too. Unlike humans, animals cannot tell us how they think but, if they respond to a magic trick in
50 the same way a human does, we can conclude that they experience the world in a similar way to humans. For example, humans often laugh when they have been fooled by a magic trick, and so do some orang- utans. Scientists have also discovered that when

... and can also help us to understand how other animals think.

55 magicians use sleight-of-hand tricks, Eurasian jays, a bird related to crows, can be fooled by some tricks but not by others. It is thought that this is because birds do not have thumbs and, as a result, magic tricks which depend on using the thumb to succeed do not fool them.

6 Magicians have entertained and fooled us for thousands of years with their
60 magic tricks. Now, those same magic tricks are helping us to better understand how
we, and other species, perceive the world and make decisions. Maybe that is the most
amazing trick ever performed.

Notes

fool「驚かす」 **Chimu**「チムー族」 **Seneca**「セネカ（4BCE-CE.65)」Lucius Annaeus Seneca ローマの哲学者・
悲劇作家。 **CE**「西暦」Chapter 5 の Notes 参照。 **misdirection**「ミスディレクション」（手品などで）人の注意
をわざと逸らすこと。 **deal**「(札を) 配る」 **sleight of hand**「手品，手先の早業」 **Eurasian Jays**「カケス」

🌐 Questions for Understanding

Part 1 Look at the following statements about the passage. Write T if the statement is True, and F if it is False. Write the number of the paragraph where you find the answer in the parenthesis.

1) _____ While there are many kinds of magic trick, the oldest used cups and balls.
[   ]

2) _____ Many people can be convinced that they saw something that did not happen. [   ]

3) _____ Some marketing techniques and magic tricks are similar. [   ]

4) _____ Unlike humans, animals are not fooled by magic tricks. [   ]

Part 2 Look at the following questions about the passage. Check the best answer for each.

1. What is surprising about the oldest magic tricks?

a. ☐ They were invented in Greece almost 2,500 years ago.

b. ☐ We do not understand how they were achieved.

c. ☐ Magicians fool audiences with the same tricks even now.

d. ☐ The Roman writer Seneca invented the cup and ball trick.

2. Which word has the closest meaning to the word "universal" in Paragraph 2?

a. ☐ unique

b. ☐ general

c. ☐ adaptable

d. ☐ individual

3. What is one way that a magician can control our choices?

a. ☐ By looking carefully at our faces

b. ☐ By positioning things carefully

c. ☐ By trying to predict what will happen

d. ☐ By making us hungry

4. Which of the following statements are true about animals, humans, and magic tricks? (Choose all that apply)

a. ☐ Magic tricks do not always succeed in fooling the audience.

b. ☐ Humans and animals always respond in the same way to magic tricks.

c. ☐ Birds cannot perform magic tricks because they do not have thumbs.

d. ☐ Being fooled by magic tricks can result in laughter.

🌐 Summary 1-46 💿

Fill each space with the best word from the list below.

experience performing species techniques perception misdirection

Magic is one of the oldest forms of entertainment. Magicians have been amazing us and fooling us with their tricks for thousands of years. By exploiting how we think, magicians can seem to perform things that are impossible. In reality, the magicians are using 1) _____ to fool our 2) _____ and forced choice 3) _____ to control our decisions. Now, scientists have started 4) _____ magic tricks to investigate how we, and other 5) _____, think and 6) _____ the world.

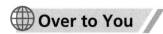 **Over to You**

Part 1 **Ask** Ask and answer the following questions.

1. Do you think magic is fun?

2. Do you know how to perform any magic tricks?

3. Have you ever been to a magic show?

4. Do you try the free samples offered at supermarkets?

5. Do you think animals enjoy playing in the same way that humans do?

Part 2 **Write** Choose ONE of the statements below. Prepare a short response giving your opinion.

- Learning how magic tricks work can improve the way we think.

- Trying to understand how animals think is a waste of time.

_____

_____

_____

_____

Part 3 **Discuss** Look at the statement below. Do you agree or disagree? Why? Share your opinion with your classmates and find out what they think.

Companies should not be allowed to use psychological tricks in order to make us buy their products.

Chapter 7

Creator or Created?

Social Media and Narcissism

Topic Activation

Think about the topic of *social media*. Write as many words connected to the topic as you can in the space below. Then, compare your words with a partner.

Useful Words

Choose a word from the list below to complete each sentence.

1. The positive feedback from the lecturer gave the student a sense of _____.

2. Although she agreed to the transfer, her _____ to go was obvious.

3. Investing in stocks and bonds is a(n) _____ risky activity.

4. He is _____ with online games. He spends all his free time playing them.

5. He said he liked my new hairstyle, but he didn't mean it. He was being _____.

obsessed	reluctance	inherently	insincere	validation

Reading

1-47 ~ 53 CD

47 CD

1 Social media is increasingly playing a major role in society. Many people spend hours every day on different platforms. Collecting selfies, inspirational quotes, and cute videos for profiles can be fun, and putting them all together to create the best image of themselves can make people feel really good. There are even people who

5 make a living being social media "creators" and "influencers." But there is one question that should be asked: when people create a social media profile, what is actually being created?

48 🎧 CD

2 Social media encourages people to display their lives to the world. Consequently, what people post is very meaningful and important to them. By making 10 posts that generate likes and shares, users can feel appreciated and gain a sense of achievement and acknowledgement that is often difficult to find in the offline world. However, while showing your life and seeking attention may seem harmless, people should think about the impact social media has on their mental health. For example, while research has found that nearly 50 percent of young people who use social media 15 feel better after using it, it has also found that 10 percent feel worse. One reason for this is the comparison and competition that social media encourages. Furthermore, the importance being placed on the search for recognition and validation can promote actions that lead to negative results. One of these results is a rise in narcissistic behavior.

49 🎧 CD

20 **3** In general terms, narcissism is a personality trait that everyone has, like reliability, empathy, and optimism. It is measured using a 40-point scale called the Narcissistic Personality Inventory (NPI), and people who score 20 or above are classified as narcissists. Studies published in the *Journal of Personality* reported that the number of young people that this applies to is rising. *Psychology Today* reported 25 that more than 10 percent of people in their 20s are believed to display narcissistic behavior. One of the proposed reasons for this is the growth in use of social media platforms.

50 🎧 CD

4 Social media is perfect for narcissists as they prefer shallow relationships that do 30 not require them to deeply consider the feelings of others. They can also post just the most attractive parts of their lives and create the illusion of always being extremely happy and successful. However, 35 social media not only attracts narcissists,

People post the most interesting images of themselves

but also creates them. Research has shown that higher amounts of social media use is correlated with higher levels of narcissism. In a 2018 study, participants who posted large quantities of photos and selfies over a four-month period showed a 25 percent increase in their NPI scores. In a society where people would rather take photos of the

40 pancakes they have ordered than actually enjoy eating them, this may not come as a surprise. Furthermore, a study conducted in Germany found that narcissists have a higher risk of developing an addiction to Facebook than those not classified as narcissists.

51 🎧 CD

5 This link is important as narcissistic behavior

45 can be very dangerous. Between 2011 and 2017, more than 250 people died while taking selfies, for example. But narcissists are not only harmful to themselves; their behavior can also be damaging to society, too. Narcissists are often self-obsessed, show

50 very little empathy, and constantly seek attention from others. Narcissists are also more likely to engage in online bullying, blame others for their own failures, react aggressively to criticism, and show reluctance to cooperate if they are not in charge.

52 🎧 CD

55 **6** In response to the increase in narcissism and its link to social media, some social media platforms are starting to make changes. In 2019, in an attempt to reduce competition among users, Instagram began

Is taking selfies narcissistic?

hiding likes from public view. Also in 2019, Instagram and the National Eating

60 Disorders Association collaborated in launching the *#ComeAsYouAre* campaign, which encouraged young people to accept their bodies as they are in order to help reduce issues surrounding eating disorders. But is this enough?

53 🎧 CD

7 It can be argued that social media is simply a tool and as such it is inherently neither good nor bad. Also, social media can be put to a range of good uses, such as

65 helping family and friends stay in touch, making support groups more accessible, and allowing people to connect for positive causes. The problem is that social media has

also helped to create a large number of narcissists, obsessed with instant happiness, self-promotion, and insincere engagement. This means that we need to be aware that while creating content can boost our self-esteem, we might also be changing ourselves
70 in ways that we do not want, which could lead to long-term negative effects that come at a high price.

🌐 Questions for Understanding

Part 1 Look at the following statements about the passage. Write T if the statement is True, and F if it is False. Write the number of the paragraph where you find the answer in the parenthesis.

1) _____ *Psychology Today* reported that the number of young people classified as narcissists is rising.　　　　　　　　　　　　　　　　　　[　　]

2) _____ Narcissists post all parts of their lives on social media platforms.　[　　]

3) _____ Narcissists work better in groups when they are in charge.　　　[　　]

4) _____ Instagram hid likes from public view to discourage direct competition.

[　　]

Part 2 Look at the following questions about the passage. Check the best answer for each.

1. What can motivate people to post on social media?

    a. ☐ They want to share pictures of the food they eat.

    b. ☐ They do it to improve their NPI score.

    c. ☐ They do it to feel appreciated.

    d. ☐ They enjoy the difficulty of making new content.

2. What is true about narcissists?

a. ☐ They feel happy after using social media.

b. ☐ They have a high score on the NPI.

c. ☐ They are usually in their 20s.

d. ☐ They often suffer from eating disorders.

3. Which word has the closest meaning to the word "illusion" in Paragraph 4?

a. ☐ trick

b. ☐ image

c. ☐ reflection

d. ☐ accusation

4. What is **not** mentioned as a benefit of social media?

a. ☐ Helping family and friends stay in touch

b. ☐ Making support groups more accessible

c. ☐ Allowing people to connect for positive causes

d. ☐ Acknowledging social media narcissism is increasing

🌐 Summary   1-54 CD

Fill each space with the best word from the list below.

addiction	aspects	consequences	imperative	support	written

The large majority of people who use social media sites enjoy the positive
1) _____ that they bring. However, there are serious 2) _____ of
over-use and an over-focus on these platforms. The positives brought by social media
can help people communicate and find 3) _____ in difficult times. The
negatives can include encouraging people to compete with their online "friends,"
promoting self-obsession, and the development of a(n) 4) _____ to looking at
their phones or computer screens. While having a break from work and checking our
profiles and the comments people have 5) _____ can make us feel good, it is
6) _____ that we consider the impact our actions are having on our mental
health.

Over to You

Part 1 Ask and answer the following questions.

1. What kinds of social media do you use?

2. How often do you use social media?

3. Do you post pictures or videos on social media?

4. Could you tell me about your worst social media experience?

5. Could you tell me about your best social media experience?

Part 2 (Write) Choose ONE of the statements below. Prepare a short response giving your opinion.

- Parents should limit how much time children spend using social media sites.
- Companies should check applicants' social media profiles before hiring them.

_____

_____

_____

_____

Part 3 Look at the statement below. Do you agree or disagree? Why? Share your opinion with your classmates and find out what they think.

The problems caused by using social media are greater than the benefits of using social media.

Chapter 8

The Man With a Pig's Heart

What Is Xenotransplantation?

🌐 Topic Activation

Think about the topic of *surgery*. Write as many words connected to the topic as you can in the space below. Then, compare your words with a partner.

🌐 Useful Words

Choose a word from the list below to complete each sentence.

1. Many people _____ money or time to charities and NPOs.

2. You used my credit card without my _____! How could you be so unethical?

3. His course is very popular, so you should _____ quickly if you want to join it.

4. She said that _____ 200 people are coming to the lecture, but it could be more.

5. Because I caught influenza, I had to _____ the date of my flight home.

| consent | register | approximately | donate | alter |

🌐 Reading

1-55 ~ 62 CD

55 CD

1   David Bennett, an American, died on March 8, 2022, due to heart failure. Nearly 700,000 Americans die from heart failure every year, so this was not an unusual event. However, Bennett's heart was unique because it was not a human heart. In January

2022, Bennett became the first person to receive a modified pig's heart to replace his own damaged heart. The use of animal organs to replace human ones, such as in this case, is called xenotransplantation and, while it could potentially save many lives, it also raises important ethical questions.

2 Why are doctors trying to transplant animal organs into humans? Many diseases can damage our organs, which can seriously affect our health and the quality of our lives. For example, damage to our hearts or lungs can make it difficult to do any physical activity. As a result, people suffering from organ failure have a high risk of dying. While scientists are learning how to grow new organs in the laboratory and are also developing mechanical replacements for some organs, it will be many years before these technologies are ready. This means that currently there is only one way for people who need a new organ to get one, and that is to receive it from another person.

3 It is possible to donate some organs, such as kidneys, while we are alive because we have two of them. But this is not possible with organs like the heart, which means that most organs for transplant must be taken from people who have died. Furthermore, these organs must be collected very soon after death has occurred. This can only be done with the consent of the patient, such as by registering as an organ donor, or of their family.

4 Unsurprisingly, most people do not like thinking about dying and so they do not register as organ donors or discuss this possibility with their families. In addition, some religions have rules and traditions that make organ donation difficult. Consequently, there are too few organ donors to provide organs for all the people who need them. In the US, about 30,000 people receive organ transplants every

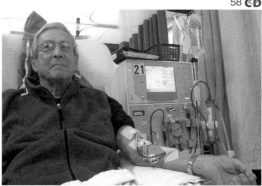

People waiting for a new kidney must endure hours of dialysis every week

year, but 100,000 need them. In Japan, only 400 of the approximately 15,000 people needing a new organ every year are able to receive one. One result of this shortage of

35 replacement organs is that many people who need one will die. Xenotransplantation is one way that this problem could be solved.

59 🎧

5 Unfortunately, it is not possible to simply transplant an animal organ into a human. Our bodies have immune systems which are incredibly effective at identifying and destroying cells which are different from our own. Consequently, when 40 performing a transplant between two people, it is necessary to make sure they match as closely as possible to reduce the risk of rejection. This means that, unless the transplant is between identical twins, most people who receive an organ transplant will need to take drugs that reduce the activity of their immune systems for the rest of their lives. But even with powerful immune suppressing drugs, an animal organ 45 transplanted into a human body will usually be destroyed in a few hours. For xenotransplantation to be successful, the animal organ must be altered so that it will be accepted by the human body.

60 🎧

6 However, to change an animal's organ so that it will be accepted by a 50 human body requires genetically modifying the whole animal. The pig that provided Bennett's heart had been modified to remove four pig genes and add six human genes. In addition, such animals 55 cannot be raised on a farm. They must be raised in a sterile environment to prevent animal viruses from being transferred to the human patient. In fact, it is likely that a

Pigs are likely to be the source of xenotransplants because their organs are similar in size to human organs

pig virus caused Bennett's death. While the virus could not infect human cells, 60 Bennett's immune system was too weak to prevent it from damaging the pig cells, causing the transplanted heart to die.

61 🎧

7 Viral diseases such as influenza, SARS, and Ebola all originated in animals. As a result, we must carefully consider the risk of new diseases resulting from xenotransplantation. Xenotransplantation also has other ethical implications. In a time 65 when many people are questioning the morality of raising animals to eat, we must ask ourselves if raising animals so that we can use their organs is ethical. Furthermore, while adding a few human genes to a pig in order to prevent immune rejection will not result in super-smart pigs or half-human monsters, it is important to consider whether it is acceptable to modify animals in this way for our benefit.

70 **8** Every year, hundreds of thousands of people die while waiting for an organ transplant. Xenotransplants are one way to help reduce the number of deaths until better technologies are developed. However, xenotransplantation raises serious ethical questions that we must consider before allowing it to become part of medical practice. Consequently, as currently the only source of human organs for transplant is other 75 humans, registering as an organ donor is perhaps something we should all consider doing.

Notes

xenotransplantation「異種間移植手術」特に動物の臓器を人間に移植すること。 **heart failure**「心不全，心臓麻痺」 **kidney**「腎臓」 **immune systems**「免疫システム」 **rejection**「拒絶反応」 **genetically**「遺伝子的に」 **sterile**「無菌の，殺菌の」 **viral**「ウィルス性の」 **SARS**「サーズ」重症急性呼吸器症候群。2003 年に世界的に流行した。 **Ebola**「エボラ出血熱」

🌐 Questions for Understanding

| **Part 1** | Look at the following statements about the passage. Write T if the statement is True, and F if it is False. Write the number of the paragraph where you find the answer in the parenthesis. |

1) _____ Nearly 700,000 Americans received modified pig's hearts in 2022. [   ]

2) _____ Most transplanted organs are taken from dead people. [   ]

3) _____ If a man needs a kidney transplant, his twin sister is the best donor. [   ]

4) _____ Ten human genes had been changed in the pig's heart Bennett received.

[   ]

| **Part 2** | Look at the following questions about the passage. Check the best answer for each. |

1. What is xenotransplantation?

a. ☐ It is the transplantation of human organs into animals.

b. ☐ It is the transplantation of animal organs into humans.

c. ☐ It is the transplantation of organs from one living person into another.

d. ☐ It is the transplantation of organs from a dead person into a living person.

2. Which of the following statements about organ transplants is correct?

a. ☐ Around one in four Japanese people who need an organ transplant will get one.

b. ☐ Americans are more likely to donate organs for organ transplant than Japanese people.

c. ☐ Most new organs are grown in the laboratory by scientists before being transplanted.

d. ☐ David Bennett was the first American to receive a mechanical replacement heart.

3. Which word has the closest meaning to the word "incredibly" in Paragraph 5?

a. ☐ hardly   b. ☐ totally   c. ☐ severely   d. ☐ extremely

4. Which of the following statements are true about xenotransplantation? (Choose all that apply)

a. ☐ Our immune systems are incredible, but they make xenotransplantation impossible.

b. ☐ Xenotransplantation requires the creation of half-human monsters.

c. ☐ It is possible that xenotransplantation could cause humans to catch animal diseases.

d. ☐ Increasing the number of organ donors may be a better alternative to xenotransplants.

Summary

1-63 CD

Fill each space with the best word from the list below.

ethical	currently	infect	modified	affect	shortage

There is a 1) _____ of organs for transplant which means that 2) _____ most people who need one will die. One possible solution to this problem is to transplant 3) _____ organs from animals. However, there are many 4) _____ problems with this idea. Another problem is that this could allow animal viruses to 5) _____ humans. We must think carefully about how xenotransplantation might 6) _____ society before allowing it to go ahead.

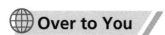 **Over to You**

Part 1 **Ask and answer the following questions.**

1. What is your blood type?

2. Have you ever donated blood?

3. Have you ever broken a bone?

4. Have you ever stayed in a hospital?

5. Would you like to work in a hospital?

Part 2 **Choose ONE of the statements below. Prepare a short response giving your opinion.**

> • Everybody should register to be an organ donor.
>
> • Some medical treatments are too expensive.

_____

_____

_____

_____

Part 3 **Look at the statement below. Do you agree or disagree? Why? Share your opinion with your classmates and find out what they think.**

> Putting an animal's organ into a human body makes you less human.

Not Just a Flu Shot

How Vaccines Have Changed Our Lives

🌐 Topic Activation

Think about the topic of *health*. Write as many words connected to the topic as you can in the space below. Then, compare your words with a partner.

🌐 Useful Words

Choose a word or phrase from the list below to complete each sentence.

1. I hate getting sick, so I get the influenza _____ every winter.

2. Unfortunately, I haven't met her yet. We've only _____ each other online.

3. Teenagers can _____ some sounds that adults cannot hear.

4. When they are told about a test, the students always _____ and start to panic.

5. The disease spread around the world in only two months. It had become a(n) _____.

pandemic	interacted with	vaccine	overreact	detect

🌐 Reading   1-64 ~ 71 📀

64 📀

1 For most of human history, people lived in small groups that only interacted with other groups of people a few times a year. This meant that, death from infectious diseases was rare, although deaths resulting from parasites was common. However, about 10,000 years ago, people began farming and living in larger groups. As a result,

⁵ new diseases emerged, and deaths caused by infectious diseases rapidly increased. Consequently, fighting infectious diseases has been an important part of the development of medicine, and vaccines are a key part of that fight.

65 CD

2 Throughout our lives, our bodies encounter many different kinds of bacteria and viruses. Most of these are completely harmless. Some, such as those that live in our ¹⁰ stomachs, are helpful. However, a very small number of these viruses and bacteria can be dangerous. Fortunately, we have very effective immune systems that can detect and destroy dangerous infections. Our immune systems work best when we are fit and healthy, which is one reason why doing plenty of exercise and eating well is so important. So, why do we need vaccines?

66 CD

¹⁵ **3** Being fit and healthy means that we are less likely to get sick and, if we do, we are less likely to suffer from a serious illness and will recover more quickly. Unfortunately, being fit and healthy is not enough to fully protect us from infectious diseases. ²⁰ One reason is that sometimes our immune systems overreact when they fight against a disease, and this can be deadly. During the COVID-19 pandemic, such immune overreactions caused many deaths, for example. Another reason is that a disease that usually ²⁵ causes a mild illness can have serious consequences. For example, in healthy children measles is usually a mild disease. However, a mild disease does not mean it is safe, and measles kills around 0.3 percent of

It isn't fun, but getting vaccinated can save your life and help to keep you healthy

healthy children who catch it. In countries where children do not get enough good ³⁰ food to eat, measles can kill nearly 30 percent of children who catch it. Furthermore, measles damages the immune system, so after catching it you are more likely to catch other diseases, even if you have had them before. Finally, around two people in every 10,000 who catch measles will later develop a fatal form of brain damage. However, being vaccinated against measles reduces the risk of death to almost zero and protects ³⁵ the immune system from the damage that measles causes.

56

Chapter 9 Not Just a Flu Shot

67 CD

4 Vaccines work by allowing our immune systems to learn about a dangerous disease in a safe way. This is usually done by presenting the immune system with bacteria or viruses that have been weakened or killed. Sometimes just a part of a virus is enough. By learning about the disease in this way, our immune systems can react

40 more quickly, which means we are less likely to get sick at all, but if we do, we will usually only experience a mild illness. This also means that we are less likely to pass the infection on to other people, which protects people who cannot get the vaccine, such as babies, people with weak immune systems, and people who are allergic to the vaccine ingredients.

68 CD

45 **5** Vaccination has been so successful in reducing deaths from infectious disease that it is sometimes difficult to understand how dangerous and terrifying some diseases can be. For example, one disease, smallpox, killed at least 100 million people between 1900 and 1980. However, an

50 international program of vaccination during the 1960s and 1970s means that today the disease has been eradicated.

69 CD

6 Paradoxically, the incredible success of vaccines in reducing deaths and disability from infectious diseases has resulted in some people coming to believe that they are

55 unnecessary or even dangerous. In some cases, this is because people overestimate the risk of very rare side

The success of vaccines means you will never suffer from smallpox

effects caused by vaccines and underestimate the dangers of the diseases they prevent. In other cases, people distrust governments and the pharmaceutical companies that make vaccines because of their unethical behaviour. However, some people actively

60 spread incorrect information about vaccines. This is often because they lack knowledge about how vaccines work and why they are important, but there are also people who spread lies about vaccines to make money.

70 CD

7 Unfortunately, such anti-vaccine ideas can be dangerous. For example, the spreading of misinformation about the measles vaccine in the 1990s resulted in a

65 reduction of children being vaccinated and an increase in children catching measles in

Europe and the US. In Japan, false information spread about the human papilloma virus vaccine in the early 2010s means that every year over 4,000 women die unnecessarily from cervical cancer, which is caused by the virus. In Sweden, by contrast, cases of cervical cancer in vaccinated women have decreased by nearly 90

70 percent.

71 🎧 **CD**

8 Today, new technologies such as mRNA vaccines, mean that vaccines for new diseases can be developed more quickly than ever before. In addition, scientists are developing personalized vaccines that can help our immune systems attack cancers. Vaccines have saved the lives of more people than every other medical development

75 combined. However, to ensure their continued success, we must fight against vaccine misinformation as strongly as we fight against disease.

Notes

infectious diseases「伝染病, 感染症」 **parasite**「寄生生物」 **immune system**「免疫システム」 **fit**「体調が良い」 **measles**「麻疹」 **smallpox**「天然痘」 **side effect**「（薬品類による）副作用」 **pharmaceutical company**「製薬会社」 **human papilloma virus**「ヒト乳頭腫ウィルス」 **cervical cancer**「子宮頸がん」 **mRNA vaccine**「メッセンジャー RNA ワクチン」 messenger RNA vaccine の略。分子を応用した新しいタイプのワクチン。

🌐 Questions for Understanding

Part 1 Look at the following statements about the passage. Write T if the statement is True, and F if it is False. Write the number of the paragraph where you find the answer in the parenthesis.

1) _____ Deaths caused by parasites became common when people began farming. [   ]

2) _____ Being fit and healthy means that we do not have to worry about disease. [   ]

3) _____ Catching measles means that you will probably catch another disease. [   ]

4) _____ Some vaccines can protect us from developing some kinds of cancer. [   ]

Part 2 Look at the following questions about the passage. Check the best answer for each.

1. Why should healthy children get vaccinated against measles?

    a. ☐ To reduce the chance of an immune overreaction to almost zero.

    b. ☐ Because measles kills nearly 30 percent of healthy children who catch it.

    c. ☐ To reduce the risk of damage to the immune system to almost zero.

    d. ☐ Because 10,000 children a year develop brain damage caused by measles.

2. Which word has the closest meaning to the word "paradoxically" in Paragraph 6?

    a. ☐ mysteriously   b. ☐ enigmatically   c. ☐ mystifyingly   d. ☐ surprisingly

3. Why do some people spread incorrect information about vaccines?

    a. ☐ Because it is no longer necessary to receive vaccinations against infectious diseases.

    b. ☐ Because vaccines killed at least 100 million people between 1900 and 1980.

    c. ☐ Because they do not have a good understanding of how vaccines work.

    d. ☐ Because of the incredible success of vaccines in reducing deaths and disability.

4. Which of the following statements about the human papilloma virus vaccine is **not** correct?

    a. ☐ The human papilloma virus vaccine causes cervical cancer.

    b. ☐ The number of cases of cervical cancer in Sweden has dropped.

    c. ☐ Several thousand Japanese women die of cervical cancer every year.

    d. ☐ Misinformation about the human papilloma virus vaccine was spread.

Summary

1-72 CD

Fill each space with the best word from the list below.

underestimate	infectious	unethical	infection	disability	fatal

Today, we rarely worry about the 1) _____ diseases that our grandparents feared. Vaccines have been so successful in reducing death and 2) _____ that some people now 3) _____ how dangerous a(n) 4) _____ can be. As a result, they would rather risk catching a disease that could be 5) _____ than get vaccinated against it. While getting vaccinated or not is a personal choice, some people spread lies about vaccines. This 6) _____ behaviour can increase the number of people who die or suffer serious harm from a disease.

🌐 **Over to You**

Part 1 (Ask) **Ask and answer the following questions.**

1. Are you afraid of needles?

2. Do you have any allergies?

3. Do you go for regular medical check-ups?

4. Have you ever tried any alternative health therapies?

5. What do you think is the most serious health problem in Japan?

Part 2 (Write) **Choose ONE of the statements below. Prepare a short response giving your opinion.**

- Getting vaccinated is not necessary if you are healthy.
- People who do not get vaccinated are a danger to society.

_____

_____

_____

_____

Part 3 (Discuss) **Look at the statement below. Do you agree or disagree? Why? Share your opinion with your classmates and find out what they think.**

Vaccinations should be compulsory.

Chapter 10 · Bad Air

The Hidden Dangers of Air Pollution

🌐 Topic Activation

Think about the topic of *pollution*. Write as many words connected to the topic as you can in the space below. Then, compare your words with a partner.

```
┌─────────────────────────────────────────────────────────────────┐
│                                                                   │
│                                                                   │
│                                                                   │
│                                                                   │
└─────────────────────────────────────────────────────────────────┘
```

🌐 Useful Words

Choose a word or phrase from the list below to complete each sentence.

1. The population in rural areas has decreased _____ in recent years.

2. There are many benefits _____ regular exercise.

3. If our good sales continue, our revenue could _____ $2 million this year.

4. There is always a lot of _____ in the air in Japan from February to April.

5. Governments around the world are _____ policies to try and reduce pollution.

associated with	implementing	pollen	significantly	surpass

🌐 Reading 1-73 ~ 79 🔵

73 🔵

1 Around the world, the number of people who smoke tobacco has significantly decreased over recent decades. In the early 1970s, over 40 percent of people in the US and UK smoked. That figure is now under 14 percent. In Japan the figure remains higher at just over 20 percent, but the number of smokers in Japan has also drastically
5 fallen. One of the main reasons for this is an increased awareness that breathing in

chemicals and smoke is very bad for our health. However, smoking tobacco is a personal choice. What about the dangers associated with breathing bad air that we do not have full control over?

2 The negative health impacts of air
10 pollution are very serious. Short-term effects include illnesses such as pneumonia and bronchitis, ailments like dizziness and nausea, and other discomfort such as irritation to the nose, throat, eyes, or skin.
15 Long-term effects include heart disease, respiratory disease, and damage to people's organs. According to the *State of Global Air* report, over seven million

74 ᏟᎠ

There are many serious health impacts associated with air pollution

deaths a year are linked to air pollution exposure and it is now the world's fourth-
20 largest risk factor for early death. Young children and older adults, whose immune systems tend to be weaker, are often more prone to the negative influences of pollution. As a result, 543,000 children younger than five years old die of respiratory disease linked to air pollution every year.

75 ᏟᎠ

3 The reason for these high numbers is that air pollution is hard to escape. Data
25 shows that 99 percent of the global population breathes air that contains high levels of pollutants that exceed WHO guidelines. This is up from 90 percent in 2019, although less strict standards were used then. The lack of visible smog, which means a mixture of smoke and fog, does not indicate that air is clean. Across the world toxic pollutants in the air surpass the recommended amounts both in cities and villages. So, while
30 going hiking in the countryside may seem healthy, and the air is probably less polluted than in urban areas, it may not be as healthy as we think. This is also an issue when exercising outside in cities because running next to a busy main road can actually cause our bodies more harm than good.

76 ᏟᎠ

4 However, staying inside is not the answer. Even though more deaths (4.5 million
35 in 2019) are linked to ambient (outdoor) air pollution, many people also die from issues linked to indoor air pollution (2.2 million in 2019). In fact, around 2.4 billion

people are exposed to dangerous levels of household air pollution. This is caused by using open fires or heaters fuelled by kerosene, biomass (wood, animal dung, and crop waste), and coal.

Air pollution can lead to worse pollen allergies

77 CD

40 **5** A further issue that people do not often talk about when discussing air pollution is increased pollen counts. As carbon dioxide levels rise, pollen-producing plants grow larger and produce 45 more pollen. As a result, pollen allergies are worsening. This is particularly bad for people who already suffer with asthma. Also, as some forms of air pollution have been identified as amplifiers of global warming, they are accelerating the rate at which 50 the Earth's temperature is rising. This increases the production of allergenic air pollutants, including mold, which is caused by damp conditions resulting from extreme weather and increased flooding. The warmer temperatures also lead to rising sea levels, more extreme weather, heat-related deaths, and the increased transmission of infectious diseases.

78 CD

55 **6** There is also a significant economic cost to air pollution. In the 15 countries with the highest greenhouse gas emissions, the illnesses and health issues caused by air pollution are estimated to cost more than four percent of GDP. Furthermore, a report on the Clean Air Act commissioned by the Natural Resources Defense Council (NRDC) in the US states that the financial benefits of cleaner air can be up to 32 times 60 greater than the cost of implementing clean-air policies and regulations. According to that report, cleaner air would lead to 189,000 fewer hospital admissions for cardiac and respiratory illnesses, and annual net economic benefits of up to $3.8 trillion for the US economy.

79 CD

7 While the outlook can seem gloomy, attempts are being made to tackle the issue 65 of air pollution. International organizations like the WHO and the UN are developing ways to help countries implement recommendations on household fuel consumption and introduce policies to expand clean household energy use, such as the Clean

Household Energy Solutions Toolkit (CHEST). Many governments are starting to introduce plans and guidelines that aim to reduce emissions from the energy, transport, waste management, housing, and industrial sectors. Also, millions of people every day are making changes in their lives, such as taking public transport, riding bikes, and buying products locally to cut down on the fossil fuels needed to transport food and other goods over long distances. If this work continues and expands, it may be possible to reduce the negative impact of the hidden dangers of air pollution.

70

Notes

pneumonia「肺炎」 **bronchitis**「気管支炎」 **ailments**「(慢性の) 病気, 疾患」 **irritation**「炎症, 痛み」 **respiratory disease**「呼吸器疾患」 **prone to**「〜の傾向がある」通例好ましくない事について用いる。 **WHO**「世界保健機関」World Health Organization の略。 **ambient**「周囲の, 取り巻いている」 **kerosene**「灯油」 **biomass**「バイオマス」エネルギー供給源とみなされる有機体。 **dung**「(家畜などの) 糞, 肥し」 **asthma**「喘息」 **the Natural Resources Defense Council**「天然資源防護協議会」 **cardiac**「心臓の」 **the Clean Household Energy Solutions Toolkit** 「家庭用クリーンエネルギーソリューションズツールキット」家庭の大気汚染や健康への影響を分析するための取り組み。WHO が開発した。

🌐 Questions for Understanding

Part 1 Look at the following statements about the passage. Write T if the statement is True, and F if it is False. Write the number of the paragraph where you find the answer in the parenthesis.

1) _____ People do not have full control over whether they smoke tobacco. [   ]

2) _____ Air pollution causes short-term and long-term negative health impacts.
[   ]

3) _____ More people died from issues linked to indoor air pollution than from ambient air pollution in 2019. [   ]

4) _____ The financial benefits of cleaner air can be greater than the cost of clean-air policies. [   ]

Part 2 Look at the following questions about the passage. Check the best answer for each.

1. Which word has the closest meaning to the word "respiratory" in Paragraph 2?
   a. ☐ breathing
   b. ☐ bodily
   c. ☐ extreme
   d. ☐ living

64

2. What was true in 2019? (Choose all that apply)

a. ☐ Ninety-nine percent of the global population breathed air containing levels of pollutants exceeding WHO guidelines.

b. ☐ Ninety percent of the global population breathed air containing levels of pollutants exceeding WHO guidelines.

c. ☐ The WHO used less strict guidelines than it does now.

d. ☐ There was a lack of visible smog.

3. What is **not** a result of rising carbon dioxide levels?

a. ☐ More people discussing increased pollen counts

b. ☐ Pollen-producing plants growing larger

c. ☐ Pollen-producing plants producing more pollen

d. ☐ Pollen allergies worsening

4. What is the Clean Household Energy Solutions Toolkit an example of?

a. ☐ An international organization like the WHO and the UN

b. ☐ A policy aimed at expanding clean household energy use

c. ☐ An emission from the energy, transport, waste management, housing, and industrial sectors

d. ☐ An everyday change people can make in their lives

Summary
1-80

Fill each space with the best word or phrase from the list below.

exposure	infectious	irritation	pollutants	prone to	regulations

The impacts of air pollution are extensive and well-known with 1) _____ to polluted air being a major factor for early death. There are also other negative health effects like pneumonia, dizziness, and 2) _____. This is particularly true for those 3) _____ poor health. However, there are some dangers connected to high levels of 4) _____ in the air that are less well-known. These include worsening allergies and increased transmission of 5) _____ diseases. To counter this governments are implementing new 6) _____, and many people are also making changes in their lives.

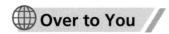 **Over to You**

Part 1 Ask and answer the following questions.

1. Does your hometown have much pollution?

2. What is the most polluted place you have been to?

3. What is the least polluted place you have been to?

4. Do you do anything to reduce your impact on the environment?

5. What is the biggest environmental concern in your area?

Part 2 Choose ONE of the statements below. Prepare a short response giving your opinion.

> • Companies have a bigger impact on the environment than individuals.
>
> • We should always buy eco-friendly products.

_____

_____

_____

_____

Part 3 (Discuss) Look at the statement below. Do you agree or disagree? Why? Share your opinion with your classmates and find out what they think.

> Protecting the environment should be the top priority for governments.

Chapter 11

Marketing Mistakes

When Advertising Doesn't Pay

🌐 Topic Activation

Think about the topic of *advertising*. Write as many words connected to the topic as you can in the space below. Then, compare your words with a partner.

🌐 Useful Words

Choose a word or phrase from the list below to complete each sentence.

1. In an attempt to _____ the man wore a red suit to the ceremony.

2. The company _____ for the error.

3. The students felt that the teacher's criticism of their presentation was _____.

4. The man's boss _____ him of stealing.

5. The supporters' actions were aggressive and _____.

| accused | apologized | confrontational | harsh | stand out |

🌐 Reading   2-01 ~ 06 CD

01 CD

1 Have you ever had an idea that seems perfect when you think of it? Sometimes we can be lucky and that idea will prove to be successful, solving a problem or making our lives better in some way. Other times we can look back at that idea and it will seem awkward, misguided, or just wrong. This does not only happen in our
5 personal lives, it also happens to companies and their marketing departments. In fact,

there have been many cases of advertising campaigns going badly and damaging the image of a brand instead of promoting it. When companies start to develop a marketing plan, they want to create impactful campaigns that stand out. They never intentionally want to insult or hurt people, but sometimes that is exactly what happens.

02 🎧 ⓒⒹ

10 **2** There are many reasons why advertising campaigns fail, but one of the most significant factors is insensitivity. One of the most damaging examples of this is racial insensitivity. For example, in 2016, Sony promoted its white PlayStation Portable device with an advertisement showing a white-haired white woman grabbing a black woman by the face with the slogan, "PlayStation Portable. White is Coming." Many 15 people were upset with this confrontational imagery. Another example was Dove's 2017 advertisement which was perceived by some as showing a young African American woman transforming into a white woman after using its body wash. Dove apologized and said the advertisement was intended to show "the diversity of real beauty." However, it still received very bad reviews and publicity. Another 20 unfortunate example was when Nivea posted an image with the text, "White Is Purity." This was interpreted as racially insensitive and was even adopted by white supremacist groups online.

03 🎧 ⓒⒹ

3 There have also been famous cases of gender insensitivity. On International Women's Day in 2021, Burger King published a Twitter thread which began with a 25 tweet that said, "Women belong in the kitchen." This was followed by two more tweets. The first said, "If they want to, of course," and the second announced their new scholarship program to help women get a degree in culinary arts and reduce the gender gap in 30 the restaurant sector. However, many Twitter users did not read the second or third tweets, resulting in a wave of harsh criticism for the first seemingly sexist statement. Another example was an Audi commercial where a bride and groom are about to get married. 35 Before the wedding can start, the mother of the groom starts to inspect the bride. When the mother approves, after checking the bride's teeth, mouth, and

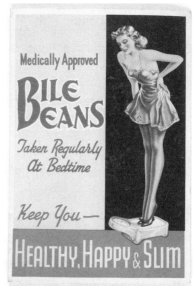

Many adverts from the past used stereotyped images

other facial features, the scene changes to a red Audi car and a man's voice says, "an important decision must be made carefully." Many people complained, claiming that
40 the advertisement objectified women and reduced their value to that of a vehicle.

4 While it is important for advertisements to connect with a target audience on an emotional level, this has to be done sensitively. McDonald's failed to
45 do this in a 2017 advertisement campaign that showed a boy asking his mother about his dead father. The boy was happy when he discovered that his father had loved the same kind of sandwich as him.

04 CD

Should companies try and profit from natural disasters?

50 McDonald's received a lot of criticism for this campaign as people accused them of exploiting a child's grief to sell sandwiches. Another example of a company being accused of using grief to profit was Facebook using Puerto Rico as the site of an online tour to promote a virtual reality app shortly after the area had been devastated by a bad hurricane season. Many people felt that Facebook was attempting to benefit
55 from the destruction and suffering that had occurred.

05 CD

5 Sometimes advertising can go beyond insensitivity and can actually be perceived as promoting dangerous or illegal activity. In 2015, Bloomingdale's, an American chain of department stores, published an advertisement showing a man staring at a laughing woman with the caption, "Spike your best friend's eggnog when they're not
60 looking." The advertisement caused outrage as it seemed to encourage drugging people without their consent. In 2017, the year the #MeToo movement began, Ford ran a campaign that featured three women who were tied up, gagged, and stuffed in the trunk of a car. The company wanted to promote the large amount of storage space their new car had, but many people found the advertisement offensive and felt that it
65 encouraged violence against women. Ford withdrew the advertisement and issued a public apology.

06 CD

6 Every company wants to stand out and look good. Creating a unique and impactful advertising campaign is a great way to do that. But if those campaigns are

not planned well, they are at risk of going viral for the wrong reasons. We all make
70 mistakes. In fact, mistakes can actually be the best opportunities for growth. However,
when mistakes that insult or hurt people are made so publicly, they can be very
damaging. So, whether a business is a huge brand or a local shop, it is important that
they present their message in an interesting, memorable, and sensitive manner.

Notes

insensitivity「無神経・鈍感」 **grab**（人）**by**…「（人）の～を掴む」 **International Women's Day**「国際女
性デー」（3月8日）1975年に女性の権利と社会参加を促進するために制定された。 **culinary arts**「料理法」
Bloomingdale's「ブルーミングデールズ」New Yorkの高級デパート。 **spike**「（気づかないよう飲み物に）アル
コールや薬物を加える」 **eggnog**「エッグノッグ」卵に牛乳，砂糖を加えた飲み物。ラム酒を入れることがあり，
クリスマスなどに皆で飲む。 **gag**「猿ぐつわをはめる」 **go viral**「バズる」インターネット上に投稿したものが
拡散されて有名になること。

🌐 Questions for Understanding

Part 1 Look at the following statements about the passage. Write T if the
statement is True, and F if it is False. Write the number of the paragraph
where you find the answer in the parenthesis.

1) _____ The Dove advertisement was adopted by white supremacist groups
online.   [   ]

2) _____ Many Twitter users only read the first Burger King tweet.   [   ]

3) _____ Facebook was accused of using a child's grief for profit.   [   ]

4) _____ Some advertisements can be seen as promoting illegal behavior. [   ]

Part 2 Look at the following questions about the passage. Check the best
answer for each.

1. What did Burger King's third tweet announce?

 a. ☐ That it was International Woman's Day

 b. ☐ That women belong in the kitchen

 c. ☐ That some women want to be in the kitchen

 d. ☐ That there was a new scholarship program

2. Which word has the closest meaning to the word "exploiting" in Paragraph 4?

a. ☐ damaging

b. ☐ improving

c. ☐ using

d. ☐ worsening

3. What did the Ford campaign want to focus on?

a. ☐ Drugging people without consent

b. ☐ The #MeToo movement

c. ☐ The storage space in a new car

d. ☐ Violence against women

4. What is important for an advertising campaign to succeed? (Choose all that apply)

a. ☐ That it is impactful and stands out

b. ☐ That it is insensitive

c. ☐ That it promotes dangerous activity

d. ☐ That it presents the message in an interesting and memorable way

⊕ Summary   2-07 💿

Fill each space with the best word or phrase from the list below.

insensitivity   insults   perceived by   publicity   significant   withdraw

A good advertising campaign can lead to 1) _____ increases in the sales of a product. However, a bad campaign which 2) _____ or upsets people can have the opposite effect. To ensure that advertisements are 3) _____ people positively they must be planned well. This includes making sure that they avoid 4) _____, especially based around race and gender. There have been many examples of large companies making mistakes and needing to 5) _____ advertisements. This shows that even though large sums of money are often invested in advertising campaigns, they can actually lead to bad 6) _____ and damage the image of a brand, not promote it.

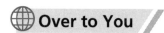 **Over to You**

Part 1 **Ask** Ask and answer the following questions.

1. Do you have a favorite advertisement?

2. Are there any advertisements that you do not like?

3. Do you watch online advertisements until the end?

4. Have you ever bought anything because you liked the advertisement?

5. Do you have an idea for a good advertisement?

Part 2 **Write** Choose ONE of the statements below. Prepare a short response giving your opinion.

- Companies spend too much money on advertising campaigns.
- Advertisements should not be aimed at children.

_____

_____

_____

_____

Part 3 **Discuss** Look at the statement below. Do you agree or disagree? Why? Share your opinion with your classmates and find out what they think.

Advertising products that are bad for our health
should be banned.

Chapter 12

Bought and Sold

Who Owns Life?

Topic Activation

Think about the topic of *ownership*. Write as many words connected to the topic as you can in the space below. Then, compare your words with a partner.

Useful Words

Choose a word from the list below to complete each sentence.

1. We need the teacher's _____ to open a maid café during the school festival.

2. Reducing tax was the government's most popular _____.

3. I can't _____ the noise you're making any longer. I'm going to the library to study.

4. My mother showed my friends some pictures of me when I was a baby. It was so _____.

5. If you do not leave the building now, the police will remove you _____.

decision	embarrassing	permission	tolerate	forcibly

Reading   2-08 ~ 14 CD

08 CD

1 For thousands of years, the buying and selling of people was an important part of many societies. Today, however, owning another person is a crime. But do we own ourselves? For example, if your friend takes a photo of you, does that picture belong

73

to you or to your friend? If your friend took the picture in a public place or if they had your permission to take it, then the picture would belong to your friend. If the picture violated your privacy in some way, however, it would belong to you. The fact that pictures taken in public belong to the photographer is why it is easy to find embarrassing pictures of famous people in the media. So, you do not necessarily own your image, but what about other information about you?

09 CD

2 Many of us enjoy using the free services offered by social media companies and internet search engines. The companies that provide these services can make huge amounts of money. For example, Alphabet, the owner of Google and YouTube, had revenues of more than $280 billion in 2022. How can a company that provides free services make so much money? The answer is that these products are not really free. The reason that social media companies provide you with free services is so that they can collect your data. This is because by collecting data from millions of people, social media companies can sell targeted advertising more effectively. In other words, social media companies make money by selling advertising that is based on your preferences.

10 CD

3 However, the data that is helpful for advertisers can also be useful for scientific research or political campaigns. While most people seem willing to tolerate being bombarded by personalized ads in exchange for useful free services, many people are less willing to unknowingly participate in scientific or political research. For example, in 2013, a company called Cambridge Analytica conducted personality research using a Facebook app. About 300,000 people took part in this research but, due to carelessness by Facebook, Cambridge Analytica was able to collect personal data from nearly 90 million people without their consent. Cambridge Analytica then used this data in political campaigns. It is important that the unethical uses of our data such as this are prevented and, in 2018, the General Data Protection Regulation (GDPR), a set of rules focusing on data protection and use, became law in the European Union. Many other countries, including Chile, Japan, and Kenya, have adopted similar laws.

11 CD

4 If we do not always own our images or our data, what about our bodies? The most basic principles of human rights are the rights to life and bodily autonomy. This means that nobody has the right to interfere with our bodies without our consent. This

35 is why getting a vaccination, donating blood or an organ, having surgery, having sex, or even having a baby must be our own decision. It is also why violations of this fundamental right, such as government

40 programs to forcibly sterilize people, are considered to be crimes against humanity.

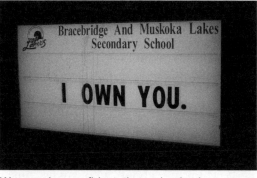

12 CD

We can be confident that schools do not own their students

5 In 1951, Johns Hopkins Hospital in the US collected cells from Henrietta Lacks without her permission and sold them to researchers around the world. Between

45 1986 and 1996, researchers at Alder Hey Children's Hospital in the UK collected organs from 850 children without the consent of their parents. Because of scandals like these, countries like the UK passed laws to ensure that our ownership of our bodies also includes parts of our bodies, even parts that will be removed and destroyed by doctors. This means that doctors must obtain our consent before beginning any

50 research using our body parts.

13 CD

6 While we definitely own our bodies, we may not own the genes that make them. In 2013, Myriad Genetics, a company which develops genetic tests for cancer,

55 patented the BRCA1 gene in Australia. This gene is found in all humans and some variants of it can cause breast cancer. A patent means that, until the patent expires,

Should companies be allowed to own our genes?

anyone who wants to make, use, or sell the patented item must get a license from the

60 patent holder. Does this mean that Myriad Genetics owns a part of all of us? Fortunately, the answer is no, but controversies like this have forced countries to think about the commercial use of biological discoveries and inventions. Ethical questions such as this have no simple answer and different countries have arrived at different conclusions. This means that in some countries, gene sequences, biological products,

65 and even genetically engineered plants and animals, such as tomatoes and mice, can be patented and owned by companies. However, most countries agree that the animals

and plants found in nature – including humans – cannot be patented. Furthermore, some countries, including Bolivia, Bangladesh, Uganda, and New Zealand, have started giving nature the same legal rights to exist and to be as free of interference as
70 people. By doing this, they hope to protect the natural world, prevent further damage to nature, and even to force companies to fix some of the destruction they have caused.

7 Thinking about who owns our data and our bodies can be complex and confusing. However, by doing so we can get a better understanding of how society
75 functions and how our rights have developed. Furthermore, by understanding how we own ourselves, we can find new ways to protect all life in the world.

Notes

bombard「（情報・質問などを）浴びせる，攻めたてる」　**ad**「広告」advertisement の略語。　**autonomy**「自律性」　**sterilize**「不妊にする」　**gene sequence**「遺伝子配列」　**engineer**「（遺伝子）を操作する」

🌐 Questions for Understanding

Part 1 Look at the following statements about the passage. Write T if the statement is True, and F if it is False. Write the number of the paragraph where you find the answer in the parenthesis.

1) _____ No one can take a picture of you unless you give them your permission.

[   ]

2) _____ Millions of people used the Cambridge Analytica app on Facebook.

[   ]

3) _____ Even parts of our bodies that have been removed by a doctor are ours.

[   ]

4) _____ In 2013, the Myriad Genetics company invented the BRCA1 gene. [   ]

Part 2 Look at the following questions about the passage. Check the best answer for each.

1. Why do social media companies provide free services? (Choose all that apply)
   a. ☐ So that they can collect our personal data
   b. ☐ To conduct personality research
   c. ☐ To help protect our right to privacy
   d. ☐ To sell advertising more effectively

2. Which of the following statements about bodily autonomy is correct?

a. ☐ People cannot use data about us without our permission.

b. ☐ Companies can patent and own our gene sequences.

c. ☐ Bodily autonomy is considered to be a crime against humanity.

d. ☐ Governments and companies cannot tell us how to use our bodies.

3. What happened at Alder Hey Children's Hospital?

a. ☐ Researchers collected children's gene sequences and sold them to companies.

b. ☐ Researchers collected children's cells and sold them around the world.

c. ☐ Researchers removed and destroyed children's body parts without consent.

d. ☐ Researchers collected children's body parts without consent.

4. Which word has the closest meaning to the word "interference" in Paragraph 6?

a. ☐ assistance

b. ☐ embarrassment

c. ☐ hindrance

d. ☐ barrier

🌐 Summary   2-15 CD

Fill each space with the best word from the list below.

gene	confusing	violate	autonomy	image	fundamental

Understanding how ownership works can be very 1) _____. While we have the 2) _____ right to privacy, this does not mean that we also own data about us, including our 3) _____. As a result, while we own ourselves, a company can own our data and even our 4) _____ sequences. Consequently, we must make sure that we do not allow companies and governments to 5) _____ our rights to privacy and 6) _____.

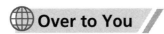 **Over to You**

Part 1 Ask and answer the following questions.

1. Do you think you share too much personal information online?

2. Has someone ever shared information about you without your consent?

3. Do you think it is okay to take a picture of someone without asking?

4. Do you think that parents own their children?

5. Who do you think owns your culture?

Part 2 Choose ONE of the statements below. Prepare a short response giving your opinion.

> • Animals should be given the same rights as people.
>
> • A picture of me should belong to me.

_____

_____

_____

_____

Part 3 Look at the statement below. Do you agree or disagree? Why? Share your opinion with your classmates and find out what they think.

> Companies should not be allowed to collect our data
> without our consent.

Chapter 13

The High Price of Poverty

What Is the Poverty Premium?

🌐 **Topic Activation**

Think about the topic of *wealth*. Write as many words connected to the topic as you can in the space below. Then, compare your words with a partner.

🌐 **Useful Words**

Choose a word or phrase from the list below to complete each sentence.

1. Student dormitories are often a much cheaper option than renting private _____.

2. If you _____ a good score on all your tests, I will take you to Disneyland.

3. I have a(n) _____ to see the doctor at 2 o'clock.

4. I have always _____ this piece of music. But I can play it now thanks to your help.

5. We can always _____ her to help us when we need it.

| rely on   obtain   struggled with   appointment   accommodation |

🌐 **Reading**   2-16 ~ 24 CD

16 CD

1 American writer James Baldwin once stated that, "Anyone who has ever struggled with poverty knows how extremely expensive it is to be poor." In economics, the idea that poor people sometimes have to spend more money than people who are not poor is called the poverty premium. But how can not having

5 enough money cause you to spend more money? By considering some different aspects of life, we can come to understand what the poverty premium is and how it can be reduced. First, however, we must understand how wealth is shared around the world.

17 CD

2 It is easy to understand that wealth is 10 not shared equally. Students and part-time workers are usually paid less than full-time workers, for example. However, learning how unequally wealth is shared in the world can be quite shocking. In 2021, the 15 richest one percent of people owned 47.8 percent of all the world's wealth. The richest 10 percent of people owned around 85 percent of the world's wealth. By

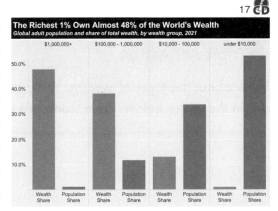

Global wealth is shared unequally (inequality.org)

contrast, the poorest 50 percent of people owned only about one percent of the world's 20 wealth. This wealth imbalance varies a lot in different countries. In Japan, the richest one percent own about 13 percent of the country's wealth, while the richest one percent in the US own 40 percent of the country's wealth.

18 CD

3 Because the distribution of wealth varies so much around the world, economists have developed two ways of defining poverty. The first is absolute poverty, which 25 means that you do not have enough money to meet your basic needs, such as food and water. Today, about 20 percent of people around the world live in absolute poverty. The second type of poverty is relative poverty, which means that you do not have enough money to meet the minimum standard of living in your country. In some countries, such as the UK, you are considered to be poor if you earn less than 60 30 percent of the average income. Now we can consider how the poverty premium can affect our lives.

19 CD

4 *The cost of money:* People living in poverty have low salaries, which means that they cannot obtain bank loans. As a result, they must rely on using credit cards and payday loans to pay for emergencies. However, while the interest rate of a bank loan 35 may be a few percent per year, short-term loans such as credit cards and payday loans are often between 12 and 30 percent per month. Consequently, someone borrowing $100 from a bank for a year may have to pay back $105, but someone relying on payday loans to do the same may have to pay back as much as $650.

20

5 *A roof over my head:* Banks will not usually give loans to people with low incomes, and this includes housing loans. This means that people living in poverty cannot buy a house and must rent their accommodation. However, accommodation with a low rent can often be of low quality and is usually far away from town or city centers.

There is poverty even in the richest countries, as this homeless man in Canada shows.

21

6 *Transport trouble:* Being forced to live on the outskirts of a town means that the journey to work takes longer and costs more money. If someone living in poverty drives a car, it will usually not be new, and is more likely to break down and require costly repairs. This can lead to days off work, missed appointments, and even more expenses.

22

7 *Food deserts:* Instant noodles are a stereotypically popular food among university students. This is because they are tasty, easy to prepare, have a long shelf life, and are cheap. However, it is not good for your health to eat such food for a long time. People living in poverty often cannot afford healthy food such as fresh fruit and vegetables. Furthermore, they may live in a food desert, an area where there are no local shops which sell fresh food. As a result, poor people can be faced with the choice of eating low-quality food or not eating at all.

23

8 *Poverty is deadly:* Living in low-quality accommodation and having a poor diet can damage your health. In addition, people living in poverty often have physically demanding jobs, or more than one job, but may not have health insurance. If they become sick, they may not be able to afford medical care or to take time away from work to recover. Furthermore, living in a financially difficult situation is extremely stressful. As a result, people on low incomes live shorter lives than wealthier people.

In the US, this difference is especially large, with the richest people living an average of 4.5 years longer than the poorest.

9 Poor people pay for their poverty with their money, their health, and their lives. However, these problems can be solved by providing good quality social housing, public transport, health insurance for all, and by paying salaries that allow people to live and not just survive. The United Nations' Sustainable Development Goal 1 is to "End poverty in all its forms everywhere." This means both at home and abroad. What can *you* do to help achieve this goal?

Notes

James Baldwin「ジェイムズ・ボールドウィン（1924-87)」米国の黒人作家。人種・セクシュアリティ・貧困など についてアメリカ社会を批判的に描いた。 **payday loan**「ペイデイローン」短期間，少額で高金利のローン。次の 給料を担保にする。 **outskirt**「郊外」 **shelf life**「貯蔵期間」 **social housing**「低価格住宅」地方自治体などが 安価で賃貸・販売する住宅。

🌐 Questions for Understanding

Part 1 Look at the following statements about the passage. Write T if the statement is True, and F if it is False. Write the number of the paragraph where you find the answer in the parenthesis.

1) _____ Wealth is shared less equally in Japan than it is in the United States.
[   ]

2) _____ Around one in five of all people do not have enough money to buy food.
[   ]

3) _____ A food desert is an area where there are no local farms producing fresh food. [   ]

4) _____ Rich people in the US live shorter lives than poor people because of stress. [   ]

Part 2 Look at the following questions about the passage. Check the best answer for each.

1. Which of the following statements about wealth inequality is correct?

a. ☐ The richest person in the US owns 40 percent of the country's wealth.

b. ☐ About one percent of the world's wealth is shared among 50 percent of the people.

c. ☐ One percent of Japanese people control about 85 percent of the country's wealth.

d. ☐ The richest 10 percent of people own nearly 50 percent of all the world's wealth.

2. What is relative poverty?

a. ☐ It means that you earn less than 60 percent of the average income in the UK.

b. ☐ It means that the poverty premium is affecting your life.

c. ☐ It means that you do not have enough money to meet your basic needs.

d. ☐ It means that you cannot afford the minimum standard of living in your country.

3. Which word has the closest meaning to the word "distribution" in Paragraph 3?

a. ☐ share

b. ☐ sequence

c. ☐ transfer

d. ☐ arrangement

4. Which of the following statements about poverty is **not** correct?

a. ☐ It can be difficult to get health insurance if you have a low income.

b. ☐ The interest rate of a payday loan can be 30 percent per month.

c. ☐ We know how to solve most of the problems caused by poverty.

d. ☐ It is difficult to obtain a credit card if you have a low salary.

🌐 Summary 2-25 CD

Fill each space with the best word from the list below.

transport	expenses	achieve	afford	affect	insurance

Living in poverty means you are always worried about how you will meet your daily 1) _____ , such as food and 2) _____ . The constant stress this causes can negatively 3) _____ your health. But if you cannot 4) _____ to pay for health 5) _____ , you will not be able to get good health care. The United Nations' Sustainable Development Goal 1 is to "End poverty in all its forms everywhere," but how can we 6) _____ this when half the people own 99 percent of the world's wealth?

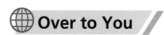 **Over to You**

Part 1 **Ask and answer the following questions.**

1. How much pocket money did your parents give you?

2. Do you have a part-time job?

3. Have you ever missed paying a bill?

4. Have you ever run out of money?

5. Have you ever borrowed money from someone?

Part 2 **Choose ONE of the statements below. Prepare a short response giving your opinion.**

- The best way to reduce poverty is to lower taxes.

- Poverty is not a problem in my country.

_____

_____

_____

_____

Part 3 **Look at the statement below. Do you agree or disagree? Why? Share your opinion with your classmates and find out what they think.**

Anyone can escape poverty if they try hard enough.

Chapter 14

Every Little Helps

How Much Money Do We Need?

🌐 Topic Activation

Think about the topic of *money*. Write as many words connected to the topic as you can in the space below. Then, compare your words with a partner.

🌐 Useful Words

Choose a word from the list below to complete each sentence.

1. Of all my _____, my monthly electricity bill is the highest. It's double my gas bill.

2. Some people think that vehicles in the future will use hydrogen as a(n) _____ instead of gasoline.

3. Getting a good education can _____ not only your life, but also your bank account.

4. When our math teacher tried to teach us English, his lack of _____ was obvious.

5. MyHomeLoan.com is the most popular _____ for people buying their first home.

expertise	utilities	enrich	fuel	lender

🌐 Reading

2-26 ~ 36

26

1 Many fairy tales end with marriage to a prince or princess. Living happily ever

after in a castle must cost a lot of money, but that's not a problem in a fairy tale. Unfortunately, most of us are unlikely to marry a prince, princess, or
5 billionaire, so we have to make our own money. How much does it cost to live happily ever after in the real world?

How much money do you have?

2 *Your home is your castle:* Whether you buy a house or rent an apartment, housing is likely to be
10 your biggest monthly cost throughout your life. The average amount people pay for accommodation in Japan is between ¥50,000 and ¥100,000 per month. Over 50 years that means you can expect to spend between ¥30 million and ¥60 million on housing. The
15 cost of insurance and your utilities, such as gas, water, and electricity, will add approximately ¥8 million more.

28 CD

3 *Driving along in my automobile:* For many people, the most convenient way to travel is by car. However, cars can cost a lot to buy and use. The lifetime cost of driving a car, including the price of the car, fuel, insurance, repairs, and maintenance
20 is between about ¥35 million and ¥65 million, depending on the type of car you drive. In other words, driving a car can cost as much as your housing.

29 CD

4 *Baby blues:* Many people look forward to getting married and having children. But the cost of raising a child is surprisingly high. According to the AIU Insurance Company, the cost of raising a child in Japan is between ¥28 million and ¥63 million.

30 CD

25 **5** *Education, education, education:* A good education can enrich our lives and help us to find better jobs. As a result, education makes up a large part of the cost of raising a child, with the cost of an education from kindergarten to university (including cram school) ranging from ¥12 million to ¥46 million.

31 CD

6 *The twilight of your life:* At the end of your career, you will probably want to
30 relax and take it easy. But will you be able to afford it? People in Japan are well-

known for their longevity, with many living into their 90s. If you retire at 65 years old, that means you will probably be retired for about 30 years. According to 35 Japan's Financial Services Agency, you will need up to ¥15 million in savings to supplement your pension during this time.

It's a lot of money, but how long will it last?

32 CD

7 *The cost of living:* Living is expensive. Today in Japan, these high 40 costs mean that around one in seven children and one in four retired people live in poverty. Living in poverty can result in poorer health and a lower quality of life. It can also result in increased levels of crime. This means that poverty is a problem for the whole of society, and we must all play our part in helping to reduce it. Something 45 that we can all do to protect ourselves from poverty is to manage our money carefully.

33 CD

8 *A penny saved is a penny earned:* Most people discover as children that it is very easy to spend money, but it is a lot harder to save it. However, saving money means that we do not have to borrow money in emergencies, and we can also earn a little money through the interest that the banks pay. A good rule of thumb is to save 50 between 10 and 20 percent of your monthly net income (the money you have left after taxes have been taken from it).

34 CD

9 *Neither a lender nor a borrower be:* Banks, credit card companies, department stores, and loan companies make it very tempting and easy to borrow money. But borrowing money to buy something means it is more expensive because you have to 55 pay interest on the loan. That is why so many businesses want to lend you money. Consequently, it is generally better to avoid borrowing money, except for a housing loan, which is unavoidable for most people.

35 CD

10 *Buy low, sell high:* Saving money is essential, but when inflation (increases in the prices of goods and services) is higher than the interest paid by your bank, the 60 value of your savings goes down. However, investing in the stock market is one way

to overcome this problem. There are two main investment strategies. The first is to try and "beat the market," that is, to choose investments that provide an above average return. The second is to "track the market," that is, to choose investments that provide an average return. The first strategy is best if you want to get rich. Unfortunately, it
65 requires a lot of expertise, knowledge, and luck because it is much easier to lose money following this strategy than it is to make it. The second strategy, investing in a low-cost tracker fund, is much less exciting and much less profitable, but also much less likely to lose you money. Investing five to 10 percent of your monthly after-tax income in one of these funds is a good target.

36 CD

70 **11** Saving money, avoiding borrowing, and making low-risk investments are not new ideas. In fact, experts have made the same recommendations for centuries. Following this advice will probably not make you rich, and cannot guarantee that you will marry royalty, but it might help you to live happily ever after. Why not start today?

Notes

a rule of thumb「実際的な目安，経験則」　**net income**「実収入」　**stock market**「株式市場」　**beat the market**「相場に打ち勝つ」市場を上回る利益を上げること。　**tracker fund**「同調資金」index fund とも言う。市場の平均株価と同じ値動きをするよう運用される投資信託。　**after-tax income**「税引後所得、実収」

🌐 Questions for Understanding

Part 1 Look at the following statements about the passage. Write T if the statement is True, and F if it is False. Write the number of the paragraph where you find the answer in the parenthesis.

1) _____ Many people spend more money on accommodation than on anything else.　　　　　　　　　　　　　　　　　　　　[　　]

2) _____ Raising a child in Japan is about as expensive as buying a house. [　　]

3) _____ Many children find that saving money is just as easy as spending it.[　　]

4) _____ Beating the investment market requires both knowledge and luck. [　　]

Part 2 Look at the following questions about the passage. Check the best answer for each.

1. Which of the following statements about housing is correct?

a. ☐ The cost of housing includes utilities and the cost of owning a car.

b. ☐ The cost of insurance and utilities increase housing costs by about one third.

c. ☐ The cost of raising a child is not included in the cost of housing.

d. ☐ Living in a castle costs between ¥50,000 and ¥100,000 per month.

2. Which of the following statements about retired life in Japan is correct? (Choose all that apply)

a. ☐ Retired people need about ¥12 million in savings to supplement their pension.

b. ☐ Retired people are advised to save between 10 and 20 percent of their salaries.

c. ☐ Around one quarter of retired people in Japan live in poverty.

d. ☐ Many Japanese people can expect to have three decades of retirement.

3. Why is it generally better to avoid borrowing money?

a. ☐ If we borrow money, we cannot get a housing loan.

b. ☐ Banks do not pay interest on borrowed money.

c. ☐ We must pay interest on money we borrow.

d. ☐ Because many businesses want us to borrow money.

4. Which word has the closest meaning to the word "strategies" in Paragraph 10?

a. ☐ projects   b. ☐ proposals   c. ☐ goals   d. ☐ systems

Summary

2-37

Fill each space with the best word from the list below.

| insurance | profitable | investments | strategies | guarantee | supplement |

Thinking about how much money you will need through your life can be scary. While it is not possible to 1) _____ that we will have enough money, there are 2) _____ that we can follow to 3) _____ our incomes. Saving regularly and taking out 4) _____ can help to protect us against emergencies.

In addition, making low-risk 5) _____ in the stock market can be
6) _____ in the long run. Following simple financial advice like this can help
to ensure that we will not end our lives living in poverty.

🌐 Over to You

Part 1 (Ask) **Ask and answer the following questions.**

1. How much money do you have with you now?

2. How much money did you spend yesterday?

3. How much money do you spend on food in a week?

4. What is the most expensive thing you have ever bought?

5. Do you save money regularly?

Part 2 (Write) **Choose ONE of the statements below. Prepare a short response giving your opinion.**

- It is better to enjoy life now than to save for the future.

- The government should do more to support children and the elderly.

_____

_____

_____

_____

Part 3 (Discuss) **Look at the statement below. Do you agree or disagree? Why? Share your opinion with your classmates and find out what they think.**

Schools should teach students about saving and investing.

Chapter 15

The Cost of Learning

What Is Education Worth?

🌐 Topic Activation

Think about the topic of *education and learning*. Write as many words connected to the topic as you can in the space below. Then, compare your words with a partner.

🌐 Useful Words

Choose a word from the list below to complete each sentence.

1. It is _____ that teachers have a big impact on students' learning.

2. In order to be fully prepared for the exam, the students took _____ classes after school.

3. In Japan, attending high school is not _____, but it is very common.

4. Working _____ is a good way to learn team-working skills.

5. Reviewing new vocabulary regularly can help _____ our understanding of it.

| collaboratively | compulsory | consolidate | supplementary | undeniable |

🌐 Reading

2-38 ~ 46 🎧

38 🎧

1 In 1990, the South African statesman Nelson Mandela said that "Education is the most powerful tool which you can use to change the world." This highlights the generally held view that education is essential in creating a brighter and more stable future, both for ourselves and for society in general. However, while there is a vast

5 range of benefits associated with learning and studying, it is undeniable that education also comes at a cost. In terms of global standards in education quality, Japan consistently ranks highly. With a literacy rate of 99 percent and a 97 percent high school graduation rate, it is clear that education is a big priority. But, is it prioritized too much?

39 CD

10 **2** *Time and Health:* In Japan, the supplementary sector of education, also known as the "shadow education sector," is very large, and very powerful. According to one study, there are roughly 15 50,000 cram schools (*juku* in Japanese) in Japan. Statista.com claims that in 2020 cram schools generated revenues of more than one trillion yen. The number of

Millions of students worldwide attend cram schools

students attending cram schools gradually increases as students progress through their 20 education and, by the third year of junior high school, 62.5 percent of students regularly attend cram schools. This takes up a lot of their time, which can impact on their physical and mental health. Being tired from cram school studies also makes it harder to focus during "regular" school lessons.

40 CD

3 *Tax:* The Japanese government invests large amounts of money in the education 25 sector in order to ensure that everyone has access to compulsory schooling. Consequently, substantial amounts of money are used to support schools and students. This enables a high standard of education to be provided and allows the large majority of children to attend. But that money must come from somewhere. As it is supplied by the government, it is funded by tax-payers' contributions. This means that childless 30 tax payers subsidize the education of other peoples' children, which they may feel is unfair.

41 CD

4 *Birth rate:* A survey on current educational costs in Japan has shown that the cost of high school education for one child is ¥2.37 million and university is ¥7.16 million, adding up to nearly ¥10 million. This figure, however, does not include cram 35 school lessons or other items such as food, clothes, and smartphones. These high educational costs can be difficult to pay. If couples feel that having children would place them under financial pressure, they may avoid having children. This could be one reason for Japan's shrinking population.

42 CD

5 *Student debt:* According to a survey conducted by the National Institute of
40 Science and Technology, 35.9 percent of graduate students who completed their master's degree in 2020 had scholarships that they were required to repay and other debts associated with their education. Approximately half of those students owed more than ¥3 million. Depending on the loan repayment plan, clearing that debt could take up to 30 years. This makes it harder to achieve financial security and reach other
45 economic goals, such as saving for retirement or buying a home.

43 CD

6 *Competitiveness:* Research has shown that getting a good education is commonly seen as a way for students to gain a competitive advantage over their peers. This departs from the concept of learning for fun and working collaboratively with classmates. If students constantly see others as rivals, it may be difficult to build
50 strong friendships. It could also increase the pressure they feel, which could lead to conflict, cheating, and lower self-esteem.

44 CD

7 *Necessity:* Some people argue that at the college and university level there are now too many degrees available. This makes it easier to gain a qualification and, as a result, reduces their value. Others claim that advances in technology are making
55 academic degrees less important in some fields, such as mapping and mathematics. It is also claimed that many qualifications do not have any practical use or relevance in the workplace. It is certainly possible to get a good job without a university education. In fact, some of the world's most successful people do not have degrees,
60 from Mark Zuckerberg, the founder of Facebook, to Richard Branson, the CEO of Virgin. So, should students be forced or pressured to study so intensely?

45 CD

8 *Over-focus:* When a large focus is
65 placed on education, attention can be taken

Can some students study too much?

away from other important areas of our lives. If we are concentrating solely on studying, can we develop our family bonds? Is it possible to stay physically and mentally healthy when all we think about is studying? Can students actually get enough time to let their minds process and consolidate the information they have
70 learned? If the answer is no, then maybe they are focusing too much on study and not enough on living and enjoying their lives.

46 CD

9 Studying and learning can help people expand their horizons and lead to more job opportunities. It can also encourage a desire for lifelong learning and enable students to make lasting friendships. However, the increasing cost and other factors
75 can have major implications both in the present and future. It is therefore essential to consider these when deciding when, where, and how much we should study.

Notes

statesman「政治家」 **Nelson Mandela**「ネルソン・マンデラ（1918-2013）」南アフリカ共和国の政治家，反アパルトヘイト運動家。同国初の黒人大統領（1994-99）となった。ノーベル平和賞受賞。 subsidize「援助する，助成する」 self-esteem「自尊心」 mapping「写像・関数」 Virgin「ヴァージン」英国のレコードレーベル。

🌐 Questions for Understanding

Part 1 Look at the following statements about the passage. Write T if the statement is True, and F if it is False. Write the number of the paragraph where you find the answer in the parenthesis.

1) _____ It is a common view that education helps create a better future. [   ]

2) _____ The average cost of university education was shown to be ¥7.16 million.
[   ]

3) _____ Approximately half of graduate students who completed master's degrees in 2020 had debts. [   ]

4) _____ Increasing education costs can impact the present and the future. [   ]

Part 2 Look at the following questions about the passage. Check the best answer for each.

1. Which of the statements about cram schools is **not** true?

    a. ☐ In Japan, cram schools make a lot of money.

    b. ☐ Cram school attendance rises as students progress through their education.

    c. ☐ Attending cram school can affect students' physical and mental health.

    d. ☐ Attending cram school can help students concentrate at "regular" school.

2. What can be provided as a result of government investment?

a. ☐ Supplementary schooling

b. ☐ A high standard of education

c. ☐ Tax-payer's contributions

d. ☐ A feeling of things being unfair

3. What is a consequence of competitiveness in education? (Choose all that apply)

a. ☐ The concept of learning for fun

b. ☐ Increased collaborative work with classmates

c. ☐ Difficulty building strong friendships

d. ☐ Higher levels of pressure, conflict, and cheating

4. Which word has the closest meaning to the word "relevance" in Paragraph 7?

a. ☐ connection

b. ☐ reality

c. ☐ success

d. ☐ use

🌐 **Summary** 2-47 💿

Fill each space with the best word from the list below.

consistently distract funded prioritized qualification self-esteem

As the Japanese government focuses on education, the country 1) _____ ranks highly in global comparisons. However, some believe that it is being 2) _____ too much and this is leading to negative consequences. The majority of students in Japan attend cram schools and there is a lot of competitiveness in education, which can lead to low 3) _____ . Furthermore, the high financial cost of education can create feelings of unfairness as it is 4) _____ by tax contributions. It can also impact on birth rates. While education does help people in many ways, it can also 5) _____ them from other important areas of life. Some are now questioning if a 6) _____ is really worth that cost.

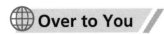 **Over to You**

Part 1 **Ask** Ask and answer the following questions.

1. What was your favorite subject at school?

2. Did you attend cram school?

3. Were your classmates at school competitive?

4. Do you think you needed to study too hard at school?

5. Do you know any successful people that did not complete university?

Part 2 **Write** Choose ONE of the statements below. Prepare a short response giving your opinion.

- Nowadays university education is not as important as it used to be.

- High school education should be compulsory.

_____

_____

_____

_____

Part 3 **Discuss** Look at the statement below. Do you agree or disagree? Why? Share your opinion with your classmates and find out what they think.

University education should be free for all students.

Chapter 16

Help or Hindrance?

The Impact of Foreign Aid

🌐 Topic Activation

Think about the topic of *charity and foreign aid*. Write as many words connected to the topic as you can in the space below. Then, compare your words with a partner.

🌐 Useful Words

Choose a word from the list below to complete each sentence.

1. Many charities need the _____ they receive to continue helping others.

2. In recent times, the population of Japan has been _____.

3. Despite greater levels of cultural understanding, stereotypes and _____ still exist.

4. Unfortunately, some areas of the world still have _____ access to education.

5. The debate participants became _____ aggressive and were asked to calm down.

| donations | inadequate | overly | prejudices | shrinking |

🌐 Reading

2-48 ~ 55 CD

48 CD

1 The idea of helping others in need is one that most people agree with. This can be seen by the large number of donations people make to charities, for example. However, on a larger scale, there is a lot of debate regarding whether countries should provide other nations with foreign aid and, if so, how much. Traditionally, most foreign aid was provided by charities. However, in 1970, the UN set a target for rich countries to donate 0.7 percent of Gross National Income (GNI) as foreign aid. Today, the majority of foreign aid, around 85 percent, comes from government sources. The largest contributor, the US, provided $35.5 billion of foreign aid in 2020, with Germany providing $28.4 billion, the UK $18.6 billion, and Japan $16.3 billion. When 80 percent of the world's population lives on a salary of $10 or less per day, why is there so much controversy about richer countries sending aid?

49 **CD**

2 One reason is that the terms "foreign aid," "humanitarian aid," and "development aid" are often used interchangeably with no official agreement on their meaning and this can cause confusion. For example, the US government mostly uses the term "foreign aid," but the British government usually refers to it as Official Development Assistance, or ODA. Additionally, people often think of foreign aid as only referring to money being sent abroad, but it also includes equipment, services, and training. The issue is further complicated by the different perceptions of the advantages it brings. So, why do countries send foreign aid?

50 **CD**

3 From an ethical perspective, it can help make the world fairer. One use of foreign aid is to improve trade relationships, which can help to increase wealth and reduce poverty, shrinking the gap between richer and poorer countries. These trade agreements can also create a better supply of food, through the development of agricultural processes, and boost the availability of important medical equipment. This can help to reduce the spread of diseases, increase average life expectancy, and lead to overall improvements in quality of life.

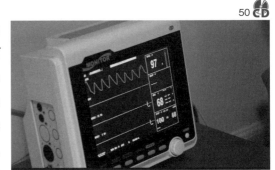
Foreign aid can increase the availability of important medical equipment

51 **CD**

4 Providing countries with foreign aid can also increase access to education, resulting in technological progress, lower unemployment rates, and better job opportunities. This means that countries can become more independent. Furthermore,

35 foreign aid can help to restore peace, reduce extremism, and combat prejudices, leading to greater levels of understanding and tolerance in global society.

5 With all of these benefits, why do some people argue against sending foreign aid? One of the most common
40 counterpoints is that large sums of money should not be given to foreign countries until major domestic problems such as homelessness, poverty, and inadequate health care are addressed. This is
45 exacerbated by the fact that foreign aid can be used inefficiently. One example of this

52

Should domestic problems like homelessness be prioritized?

is "duplication of effort." This occurs when two different organizations try to help the same area with the same problem, such as building a well, while neglecting another area that has the same issue. Also, part of the aid donated may not reach its intended
50 target due to corruption.

53

6 Furthermore, while proponents claim that small amounts of money can have a big impact, in reality the aid is often not enough to solve large structural problems. This means that receiving countries can become heavily dependent on aid. Two examples of this are Mozambique and Ghana, where the level of dependency as a
55 percentage of GDP rose by 16 and 20 percent respectively in less than 20 years since they started receiving assistance from the US.

54

7 Also, who decides where foreign aid is sent? There are many nations and people in need, but some countries are favored over others. This is an accusation commonly directed at the UK as many foreign aid watchdogs feel that it overly concentrates on
60 its former colonies. This situation can create frustration and a feeling of injustice. It is also claimed that foreign aid is often given with a hidden agenda. The countries that give foreign aid regularly make sure that they will benefit from the money they give. Sometimes, the aid is provided only when business opportunities are available. This is known as "trade for aid" and it means that the donating countries gain power in aid-
65 receiving countries. The US and China have often been criticized for this practice.

Also, as companies from donor countries enter the receiving country's economy, local businesses may lose their competitiveness and inflation can increase.

8 It is clear that foreign aid programs have helped to improve the living conditions of billions of people all over the world. Yet, many programs are inefficient and can
70 actually cause additional problems and hinder progress. From 1971 to 1994, the US donated over $1 trillion in foreign aid to help the 70 poorest countries in the world, but by 1996, the UN declared that 43 of those 70 countries were in a worse economic position than they were before they started receiving aid. Consequently, some believe that foreign aid can do more harm than good, and if not implemented properly, may
75 increase global tensions. However, while there are many drawbacks to foreign aid, when the natural desire to help others is successfully realized through aid projects, incredibly positive outcomes can be achieved.

Notes

Gross National Income「国民総所得」 **extremism**「(政治的に) 極端に走る傾向」 **exacerbate**「悪化させる」 **duplication**「重複」 **GDP = Gross Domestic Product**「国内総生産」 **watchdog**「監視者」

🌐 Questions for Understanding

Part 1 Look at the following statements about the passage. Write **T** if the statement is True, and **F** if it is False. Write the number of the paragraph where you find the answer in the parenthesis.

1) _____ Germany was the largest contributor of foreign aid in 2020. 　 [　]

2) _____ Foreign aid includes equipment, services, and training. 　 [　]

3) _____ Foreign aid can lead to greater levels of understanding and tolerance.

　 [　]

4) _____ Foreign aid commonly solves large structural problems. 　 [　]

Part 2 Look at the following questions about the passage. Check the best answer for each.

1. Which of the statements is **not** listed as a benefit of improved trade relationships?

　 a. ☐ Fairer ethical perspectives

　 b. ☐ Increased wealth and reduced poverty

　 c. ☐ Development of agricultural processes

　 d. ☐ Increased availability of important medical equipment

2. Which of the statements is **not** given as a reason against sending foreign aid?

    a. ☐ Money should be used to address domestic issues first.

    b. ☐ It can be used inefficiently.

    c. ☐ It can cause some areas to be neglected.

    d. ☐ Part of the aid donated may not reach its intended target.

3. Which word has the closest meaning to the word "agenda" in Paragraph 7?

    a. ☐ agency

    b. ☐ direction

    c. ☐ plan

    d. ☐ question

4. Which of the statements about foreign aid is true? (Choose all that apply)

    a. ☐ The UN set a target for rich countries to donate 0.7 percent of GNI as foreign aid.

    b. ☐ Most foreign aid comes from charities and international organizations.

    c. ☐ In 2020 Japan contributed more to foreign aid than the UK.

    d. ☐ The US donated more than $1 trillion in foreign aid from 1971 to 1994.

🌐 Summary 2-56 CD

Fill each space with the best word from the list below.

boost   corruption   controversial   drawbacks   regarding   tolerance

While most people agree that it is important to help others, the issue of foreign aid is still 1) _____. Foreign aid programs can help improve the lives of people all over the world. Trade agreements can 2) _____ the supply of medical equipment, which can help increase average life expectancy. Access to education and technological progress can also lead to more understanding and 3) _____. However, there are also many 4) _____. The money that has been donated can be used inefficiently and 5) _____ can mean that some of the aid does not benefit those who need it most. As a result, there is still debate 6) _____ the amount and type of foreign aid that countries should give.

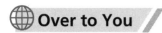 **Over to You**

Part 1 Ask and answer the following questions.

1. Do you ever donate money to charity?

2. Have you ever done any volunteer work?

3. Do you think your country donates enough money as foreign aid?

4. Where does your country send its foreign aid to?

5. Could all countries ever become equal?

Part 2 Choose ONE of the statements below. Prepare a short response giving your opinion.

> • Countries should focus on their own issues before helping other countries.
>
> • It is better to offer equipment and training as foreign aid than money.

_____

_____

_____

_____

Part 3 Look at the statement below. Do you agree or disagree? Why? Share your opinion with your classmates and find out what they think.

> Richer countries have a moral responsibility to help poorer countries.

Chapter 17

How to Change the World

Peaceful Protest

🌐 Topic Activation

Think about the topic of *politics*. Write as many words connected to the topic as you can in the space below. Then, compare your words with a partner.

🌐 Useful Words

Choose a word from the list below to complete each sentence.

1. He is a stubborn man. It is _____ arguing with him.

2. The politician was forced to _____ after the scandal.

3. The team knew they would not win the competition, but they still wanted to _____.

4. The bad weather caused a major _____ to the train service.

5. Sleeping well can _____ our ability to concentrate.

disruption	enhance	participate	pointless	resign

🌐 Reading

2-57 ~ 63 🔊

57 🔊

1 The democratic process can be frustrating as it is often complicated and inefficient. Political leaders can appear to be disconnected from the concerns of ordinary people. As a result, many people feel that voting in elections is pointless. If people feel powerless in a democracy, then that democracy has failed. But there is a
5 way that people can play a bigger role in the way their country is run. There is a way

to change the behavior of a government and political leaders outside of voting. That way is to protest.

2 If you were asked to imagine a political protest that led to a change in government, what would you think of? Guns, fighting, and violence? While these have all played a part in many revolutions around the world, protests that are non-violent are twice as likely to succeed as those that are violent. In 1986, millions of people protested peacefully in the Philippines, and after four days the

58 CD

Peaceful protests can lead to political change

government lost power. In 2003, people in Georgia entered the parliament building holding flowers, forcing the country's leader to resign. In 2019, the presidents of Sudan and Algeria both announced they would leave power. In each case, ordinary members of the public achieved large-scale political change following peaceful campaigns of protest.

59 CD

3 There are many ethical reasons to use non-violent strategies to protest. Violent protests can cause widespread damage and hurt many innocent people. However, research has found that peaceful protest is also the most successful way of creating change. It is understandable to doubt the idea that non-violent action can be more powerful than violent protest. Yet, data from hundreds of protest campaigns showed that political change was achieved in 53 percent of non-violent campaigns compared to 26 percent of violent protests. The use of non-violent protest has been endorsed and used by many influential figures throughout history, such as the anti-slavery activist Sojourner Truth, the women's suffrage campaigner Susan B. Anthony, the Indian independence leader Mahatma Gandhi, and the US civil rights campaigner Martin Luther King. But why is non-violent action more successful than other forms of protest?

60 CD

4 One reason is that more people are willing to engage in peaceful activism. Peaceful protests can include people who are against violence and fear bloodshed. In

addition, non-violent protests have fewer barriers to participation as people do not need to be in good physical health to take part. The greater variety of non-violent protest strategies means that people can participate regardless of age, gender, or
40 physical ability. Furthermore, non-violent campaigns are often more visible and easier to discuss openly. This means that they can reach a wider audience. Consequently, it is easier for people to understand the reason for the protest and to find out how to participate.

61 CD

5 The increased participation gained from engaging a much wider range of people
45 is significant. It can increase the disruption that protests create, which boosts their impact on the normal functioning of society, such as the flow of traffic in a city. Also, as more people join, the campaigns become more likely to win support among the police and the military. Overall, non-violent campaigns attract around four times as many participants as violent campaigns. This is important as research has shown that
50 if around 3.5 percent of the population are actively participating in a non-violent protest, success is almost guaranteed. This is called the "3.5% rule."

62 CD

6 Despite being twice as successful as violent protests, peaceful campaigns still fail 47 percent of the time. They also come at a personal cost as people
55 still risk being arrested. They are also not as anonymous as violent protests, which means that protestors can be identified more easily. However, the most important factor for a protest to be successful is that there must be unity among the demonstrators.
60 When campaigns become divided and protestors split into different groups, a lot of power is lost. During protests in Bahrain in 2011, the lack of cohesion that resulted from groups not working together prevented the movement from achieving change.

Demonstrators need to stay united to
63 CD *succeed*

65 **7** When the participants of a protest are committed to using non-violent strategies, more people can join and the movement becomes larger. Peaceful protests are also more likely to gain support from important

groups such as the military and security forces. This can enhance the legitimacy of what the protestors are aiming for, both domestically and internationally. This influential support increases the pressure on the groups that the protests are targeting. In addition, governments find it harder to suppress non-violent campaigns as doing so makes them look like aggressors, which often has a further negative impact on their image. Consequently, if we want to change the political environment we are living in, it is important that we start to think of ways that we can protest peacefully, encourage others to join us, and ultimately reach the 3.5 percent threshold.

Notes

Georgia「ジョージア」黒海東岸に位置する共和制国家。1991 年ソ連からの独立を宣言。首都トビリシ。 **endorse**「支持する」 **suffrage**「参政権」 **bloodshed**「流血」 **Bahrain**「バーレーン」ペルシア湾内の 30 以上の島からなる首長国。首都マナーマ。 **cohesion**「団結・結束」 **legitimacy**「正当性」 **threshold**「境界・境目」

🌐 Questions for Understanding

| **Part 1** | Look at the following statements about the passage. Write T if the statement is True, and F if it is False. Write the number of the paragraph where you find the answer in the parenthesis. |

1) _____ Other than voting, there is no way to influence a government's behavior.   [   ]

2) _____ Violence does not feature in revolutions.   [   ]

3) _____ It is more common for military and security forces to support peaceful protests than violent protests.   [   ]

4) _____ The majority of peaceful campaigns are successful.   [   ]

| **Part 2** | Look at the following questions about the passage. Check the best answer for each. |

1. Which statement is given as an ethical reason to use non-violent protest?

    a. ☐ Violent protests can cause widespread damage and hurt many innocent people.

    b. ☐ Non-violent protest is the most successful way of creating change.

    c. ☐ There is data from hundreds of protest campaigns.

    d. ☐ Many influential figures have used non-violent protest.

2. Which word has the closest meaning to the word "endorsed" in Paragraph 3?

    a. ☐ challenged   **b.** ☐ designed   **c.** ☐ supported   **d.** ☐ tackled

3. Why are more people willing to participate in peaceful activism than violent protest? (Choose all that apply)

    a. ☐ Because those who are against violence and fear bloodshed can join.

    b. ☐ Because there are no barriers to participation.

    c. ☐ Because people of any age, gender, or physical ability can join.

    d. ☐ Because they are more visible and easier to discuss openly.

4. Which of the statements is **not** listed as a potential negative of joining a peaceful campaign?

    a. ☐ People still risk being arrested.

    b. ☐ They are not as anonymous as violent protests.

    c. ☐ Other people can more easily know who is participating than in violent campaigns.

    d. ☐ There is a need for unity among demonstrators.

🌐 Summary //   2-64 💿

Fill each space with the best word or phrase from the list below.

cohesion	engage in	ordinary	regardless	strategies	suppress

When **1)** _____ people vote but they do not see any real change, they can feel powerless. This is a sign that democracy has failed. In situations like this, some feel that they have no choice but to protest. However, the methods used when protesting are important and using non-violent **2)** _____ leads to more success than using violence. This is because more people join as they can participate **3)** _____ of their personal circumstances. Once 3.5 percent of the population **4)** _____ peaceful activism, success is almost guaranteed. But, **5)** _____ is essential and the protestors must work together. If they do this, and they remain peaceful, it is more difficult for governments to **6)** _____ the campaigns.

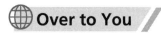 **Over to You**

Part 1 **Ask and answer the following questions.**

1. Are you interested in politics?

2. Have you ever voted in an election?

3. Do you think it is important to vote in elections?

4. Which do you read more, news about domestic politics or international politics?

5. Would you ever join a protest?

Part 2 **Choose ONE of the statements below. Prepare a short response giving your opinion.**

> • It takes too long for political change to be made.
>
> • The voting age should be reduced to 16.

_____

_____

_____

_____

Part 3 **Look at the statement below. Do you agree or disagree? Why? Share your opinion with your classmates and find out what they think.**

> People trust politicians and governments less now than
> in the past.

Chapter 18

It's My Right

How Do We Balance Competing Rights?

🌐 Topic Activation

Think about the topic of *freedom*. Write as many words connected to the topic as you can in the space below. Then, compare your words with a partner.

🌐 Useful Words

Choose a word or phrase from the list below to complete each sentence.

1. She could not believe she was pregnant until she saw a scan of her

_____.

2. The torn garbage bags were _____ that there was a bear in the area.

3. Kaori collected the prize _____ James because he was sick that day.

4. Giving children alcohol is a(n) _____ of the law.

5. This information is _____. You cannot tell anyone.

| fetus | evidence | confidential | on behalf of | violation |

🌐 Reading

2-65 ~ 71 CD

65 CD

1 Most people know that they have human rights, but do you know what your rights are? Many countries have constitutions and laws that describe the rights that their citizens have. In addition, most countries have signed international human rights agreements, such as the United Nations Universal Declaration of Human Rights.
5 While some of these agreements are voluntary, others, such as the European

Convention on Human Rights, are forms of international law. But what are human rights, and why are they important?

1949's Universal Declaration of Human Rights is the basis of human rights law in many countries.

66 CD

2 Human rights are a form of moral
10 code. That is, they describe the minimum standards of human behavior. By making it clear what kinds of behavior are acceptable, it becomes easier to recognize when we are being treated wrongly. In this
15 way, human rights laws can help protect us from the bad actions of other people, companies, and governments. However, even though we all have the same rights, there are times when our rights come into conflict with those of others. Let's consider some examples.

67 CD

3 Freedom of expression is the right to say or write or draw whatever you want.
20 This essential right allows journalists to report controversial news stories, authors to write challenging articles and books, and protestors to share their opinions. Unfortunately, many people seem to misunderstand what this right means. Complete freedom of expression means that you are free to insult your friend, tell lies about someone, harass someone online, or start a panic in a crowded place. However, if you
25 express yourself in such extreme ways, you might lose your friend, be banned from an online community, be sued, fined, or even sent to prison. In other words, freedom of expression does not mean freedom from consequences.

68 CD

4 Freedom of expression allows journalists to report important news stories.
30 However, the people and companies mentioned in those stories also have the right to privacy. This important right is why strangers cannot enter your home without your permission. This is also why
35 if the police want to search your home, they must get a court warrant to

This may not be the best way to protect your right to privacy.

110

temporarily limit your right to privacy. In addition, companies have a right to privacy, which is why you can be fired for sharing confidential business information. But how can we prevent the right to privacy from being used to hide evidence of bad behavior or criminal activity? Generally, the right to privacy can be violated if it is in the public interest. This means that society will benefit if the information becomes public. In this way, the right to privacy and the right to freedom of expression can be balanced.

69 CD

5 Even more fundamental than the rights to privacy and expression is the principle of bodily autonomy. Bodily autonomy means that no one can use your body without your consent. This principle is necessary to protect us from physical assaults ranging from sexual harassment to government eugenics programs. But what if you cannot give your permission? During medical emergencies, doctors have to make medical decisions on behalf of people who are unconscious and cannot give their consent. Most people do not consider this to be a violation of their bodily autonomy. But what about having a baby? Does a fetus have the right to use its mother's body? Deciding when a fetus has developed enough to have human rights, and whether the human rights of the mother or the baby take precedence, is incredibly difficult and often controversial. Consequently, different countries have come to different conclusions on this topic.

70 CD

6 Children have the same rights as adults. But because children do not understand the world in the same way as adults, they are usually not considered capable of giving consent to many activities that are common for adults. Instead, their parents are trusted to make good decisions on their behalf. As a minor gets closer to the age of majority (the legal age that you become an adult), their ability to give consent also increases. However, the amount of control parents have over their children and the age when children become able to make decisions can be difficult to decide, with many countries making very different decisions. Consequently, the age at which someone can have sex, get married (or divorced), get a job, get a tattoo, drive a car, vote, get a credit card, or take out a loan, can vary considerably among different countries. This can sometimes lead to some unusual situations. For example, in some US states it is possible for a teenager to be old enough to get married but too young to get divorced.

71 CD

7 Balancing human rights when they intersect with each other can be very difficult. Some of the most famous legal cases in history have focused on whose rights take precedence in a given situation. Such cases have helped to increase freedom in many countries. However, there are still countries which do not allow their citizens basic rights and freedoms, such as the right to change their religion (or to have none). Furthermore, even in the freest places, there are people and politicians who want to limit or reduce the rights of citizens in their countries. The greatest challenge for human rights is how to ensure that everyone is protected by them, even the people who want to take them away from us.

70

75

Notes

the United Nations Universal Declaration of Human Rights「世界人権宣言」1948 年 12 月 10 日に採択された。　**moral code**「道徳律」道徳的行為の規準となる法則のこと。　**news story**「新聞記事・ニュース記事」 **autonomy**「自律性」　**minor**「未成年者」　**majority**「成年」

🌐 Questions for Understanding

Part 1 Look at the following statements about the passage. Write T if the statement is True, and F if it is False. Write the number of the paragraph where you find the answer in the parenthesis.

1) _____ The European Convention on Human Rights is a kind of constitution.

[　　]

2) _____ Freedom of expression is an essential human right for journalists. [　　]

3) _____ The police are sometimes allowed to violate your human rights. [　　]

4) _____ We should only protect the human rights of people who agree with us.

[　　]

Part 2 Look at the following questions about the passage. Check the best answer for each.

1. What are human rights? (Choose all that apply)

a. ☐ They are a kind of international law.

b. ☐ They are guidelines of human behavior.

c. ☐ They are a way of identifying bad behavior.

d. ☐ They allow governments to behave badly.

2. Which word has the closest meaning to the word "warrant" in Paragraph 4?

    a. ☐ authorization

    b. ☐ law

    c. ☐ prohibition

    d. ☐ guarantee

3. Which of the following statements about the principle of bodily autonomy is correct?

    a. ☐ Companies can use it to hide evidence of bad behavior or criminal activity.

    b. ☐ It allows companies to fire you for sharing confidential business information.

    c. ☐ If someone wants to interact with your body, they must get your permission.

    d. ☐ Different countries have come to different conclusions on this topic.

4. Which of the following statements about children's rights is correct?

    a. ☐ Children have no rights until they become adults.

    b. ☐ Children gain more control over their lives as they age.

    c. ☐ Adults are not trusted to make good decisions for children.

    d. ☐ Children understand the world in the same way as adults.

Summary

2-72 CD

Fill each space with the best word or phrase from the list below.

| controversial | conflict | intersect with | constitutions | precedence | religion |

Our rights are guaranteed by international laws and national 1) _____ . When the goals of different people 2) _____ each other, human rights provide guidelines for finding a solution that maximizes the freedoms of everyone involved. However, when people express their rights, they sometimes 3) _____ with each other. For example, if a child needs medical treatment that their parents' 4) _____ does not allow, whose rights take 5) _____ ? There is often no easy answer to such questions and attempts to find a solution are often 6) _____ .

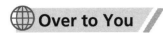 **Over to You**

Part 1 **Ask** Ask and answer the following questions.

1. Have you ever experienced online harassment?

2. How important is privacy to you?

3. Do you think it is important to vote?

4. Do you think people have enough rights?

5. What is a right you think people should have?

Part 2 **Write** Choose ONE of the statements below. Prepare a short response giving your opinion.

> • Only parents can decide what is right for their children.
>
> • Religious rules are more important than human rights laws.

_____

_____

_____

_____

Part 3 **Discuss** Look at the statement below. Do you agree or disagree? Why? Share your opinion with your classmates and find out what they think.

> People should not be allowed to say, write, or publish
> anything that could offend another person.

Chapter 19

Population Power

The Economic Impact of Immigration

🌐 Topic Activation

Think about the topic of *immigration*. Write as many words connected to the topic as you can in the space below. Then, compare your words with a partner.

🌐 Useful Words

Choose a word from the list below to complete each sentence.

1. It took the government a long time to _____ its latest policy.

2. There are a range of negative _____ associated with smoking.

3. The size of the Japanese _____ has decreased since the 1970s.

4. One _____ for studying hard is getting a good job after graduation.

5. The company's _____ increased after it introduced the new product.

| consequences | formulate | incentive | revenue | workforce |

🌐 Reading 2-73 ~ 79 💿

73 💿

1 When discussing migration, people often start with numerical data. That is because it helps us understand the scale of the movement of people from one place to another with the intention of staying there (either temporarily or permanently). It also helps us to formulate our opinions and reactions to it. The estimated number of
5 international migrants has increased dramatically over the last five decades. According to the UN, there were approximately 281 million international migrants in 2020. That

number is 3.6 percent of the world's population. It is also 128 million more than in 1990 and over three times more than in 1970. However, different countries have varying rates of net migration (the number of people entering compared to those
10 leaving). In 2019, Japan had an estimated 180,000 net migrants compared to 271,000 in the UK and 327,000 in Germany. Such large-scale international migration has many consequences, both positive and negative.

74 CD

2 One of the main reasons people migrate is for work, and this can have a significant impact on a country's economy. First, as the size of the workforce
15 increases, the amount of goods that can be produced also increases. When this is coupled with immigrants spending their wages in their new country, the greater demand for, and supply of, services and goods can help the economy grow. Also, as working immigrants pay tax on their wages, they contribute to government finances. This can reduce the extra pressure being placed on social care as a result of an aging
20 population.

75 CD

3 Immigration can also lead to a more skilled workforce. In the UK, a 2012 study found that working immigrants were more likely to have studied for longer and have
25 more qualifications than native-born workers. Furthermore, if a country has a shortage of skilled workers in a particular area, such as nurses and doctors, immigrants can fill that gap. Also,
30 immigrants can help do some types of jobs

Immigrant workers are very important in the agriculture sector

that are unpopular due to low wages and/or a negative image. For example, the agricultural sector often relies on immigrant workers. A decline in immigration to the UK in 2019 led to some farmers claiming they could not fully harvest their crops because there were not enough seasonal workers from overseas.

76 CD

35 **4** Another benefit of immigration is greater innovation and flexibility. It is argued that as immigrants often arrive with little wealth, they have a greater incentive to try and succeed. People who are willing to risk leaving a country are generally ambitious

and willing to be both flexible and dynamic. Consequently, there have been many examples of immigrants and their families becoming entrepreneurs and setting up
40 businesses which create innovative products. These include Steve Jobs (Apple), whose father was from Syria, Jeff Bezos (Amazon), the son of a Cuban immigrant, and Sergey Brin (Google), a Russian immigrant.

77 CD

5 Despite the positives, however, there are also negative impacts associated with large-scale migration. It is argued that if the majority of immigrants are unskilled,
45 overall wages in a country go down. This wage decrease tends to be greater for those with lower incomes and fewer qualifications. A 2013 study found that a one percent increase in the ratio of migrants to non-migrants led to a 0.5 percent wage reduction for the poorest 10 percent. Furthermore, if unskilled jobs are filled by immigrants because they are willing to work for lower wages, native-born low-skilled workers
50 may find it harder to gain new employment in higher-skilled occupations. This can lead to an increase in long-term unemployment.

78 CD

6 Outside of the labor market, immigration can lead to a rise in local populations which puts pressure on social
55 services and infrastructure, such as schools and hospitals. While an increase in tax revenue from immigration can increase government spending, if it is focused in particular areas, such as near borders or in
60 big cities, there can be an overall

Immigration can lead to more crowded schools

deterioration in the quality of public services provided. Further negative impacts occur when the population in an area grows too quickly. If migrants move to areas with limited housing, rents can increase, reducing living standards and increasing housing poverty. The UK government found that between 1991 and 2015 immigration had
65 contributed to a 20 percent rise in house prices, for example.

79 CD

7 The reasons for migration are an important factor when determining if the effect it has is positive or negative. This is also true for the type of work migrants do. There are also other issues not connected to economics, such as how well migrants integrate

with the local people. Therefore, as the government of a country has a responsibility to
70 look after the well-being of its citizens, finding the best way to deal with migration is
very important. However, this is a very difficult task, especially when the numbers
involved are so high.

Notes

net「正味の」　**workforce**「労働人口」　**entrepreneur**「起業家」　**deterioration**「悪化，低下」

🌐 Questions for Understanding

| Part 1 | Look at the following statements about the passage. Write T if the statement is True, and F if it is False. Write the number of the paragraph where you find the answer in the parenthesis. |

1) _____ The size of a workforce impacts the amount of goods that can be produced. [　]

2) _____ In 2019, crops in the UK could not be harvested because of too much immigration. [　]

3) _____ If the majority of immigrants are unskilled, overall wages can decrease. [　]

4) _____ There was no connection found between immigration and house prices in the UK. [　]

| Part 2 | Look at the following questions about the passage. Check the best answer for each. |

1. Which word has the closest meaning to the word "dramatically" in Paragraph 1?

   a. ☐ significantly

   b. ☐ fictionally

   c. ☐ surprisingly

   d. ☐ adequately

2. What is net migration defined as?

    a. ☐ The intention of moving from one place to another

    b. ☐ The estimated number of international migrants

    c. ☐ The number of people entering a place compared to those leaving

    d. ☐ The consequences of large-scale international migration

3. Which statement about migrants is **not** true?

    a. ☐ They often arrive with little wealth.

    b. ☐ They have little motivation to try and succeed.

    c. ☐ They are generally willing to be flexible and dynamic.

    d. ☐ Many have set up businesses which create innovative products.

4. What is listed as a consequence of immigration? (Choose all that apply)

    a. ☐ Rises in local populations putting pressure on social services and infrastructure

    b. ☐ Increases in tax revenues boosting government spending

    c. ☐ Improvement in the quality of public services

    d. ☐ Decreases in rents in areas with limited housing

🌐 Summary　　2-80 💿

Fill each space with the best word from the list below.

consider   contribute   infrastructure   integrate   significant   temporarily

Large numbers of people move to live and work in other countries, both 1) _____ and permanently. This international migration can have a(n) 2) _____ impact on the economy, the general 3) _____ , and the quality of public services that can be provided. Welcoming immigrants can have both positive and negative consequences. While many immigrants work hard and 4) _____ to society, others can find it difficult to 5) _____ with local people. As a result, it is important that governments carefully 6) _____ their immigration policies.

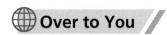 **Over to You**

Part 1 **Ask** Ask and answer the following questions.

1. Do you know any people that have immigrated?

2. Are there many immigrants in your hometown?

3. Where do the immigrants in your country mostly come from?

4. Would you ever emigrate?

5. Where do you think would be the best place to emigrate to?

Part 2 **Write** Choose ONE of the statements below. Prepare a short response giving your opinion.

- Immigrants should have the same rights as native citizens.
- Immigration is mostly good for the economy.

_____

_____

_____

_____

Part 3 **Discuss** Look at the statement below. Do you agree or disagree? Why? Share your opinion with your classmates and find out what they think.

The Japanese government should encourage more people to immigrate to Japan.

Chapter 20

Anime, Disney, and Democracy

What Is Soft Power?

🌐 Topic Activation

Think about the topic of *power*. Write as many words connected to the topic as you can in the space below. Then, compare your words with a partner.

🌐 Useful Words

Choose a word from the list below to complete each sentence.

1. When I was a child, I hated coffee, but now I _____ its flavor.

2. When we watched the video recording, we saw that he had _____ cheated.

3. I think this rule banning the use of smartphones will _____ anger among the students.

4. I'm sorry, but I could not _____ Scarlett to come to karaoke tonight.

5. Did you know that Disney has its own educational _____ called Disney University?

| appreciate | persuade | generate | institution | undoubtedly |

🌐 Reading   2-81 ~ 91 💿

81 💿

1 When you think of the United States of America, do you think of things like Hollywood and hamburgers, Disney and democracy? When you think of Korea, do you think of K-pop and K-dramas? If so, then you have experienced the soft power of

those countries. What is soft power and why is it important?

82 CD

5 **2** In general terms, power is the ability to change something or to avoid being changed. In social situations, power is the ability to achieve our goals. There are many ways that we can do this, such as persuading someone to do what we want, using threats, or even using violence to achieve our goals. Consequently, power can be described as a continuum ranging from soft (persuasion) to hard (violence). In politics,
10 power is used to change the attitudes and behavior of the people it is targeted at. Let's consider an example.

83 CD

3 If the people of a country are not satisfied with the behavior of their politicians and government, they will first use soft power, such as criticism in the media, comedy, and peaceful demonstrations. If this does not work, people might begin campaigns of
15 civil disobedience (refusing to cooperate with the government), mass protests, and other forms of direct action. Finally, the people may be forced to act violently in order to change the government.

84 CD

4 In international relations, the goal is to change the behavior of other countries. War is one way to do this, but it is very expensive, wastes human lives, and often
20 generates hatred and anger that may lead to more conflict in the future. Consequently, the use of soft power is generally preferred in diplomacy. But how does soft power work?

85 CD

5 The goal of international soft power is to encourage change in the values and
25 ideals of the citizens of a target country. This is because if the people in both countries like the same things and have the same values, they are more likely to want the same things. In this way, change
30 becomes possible without the use of

Participants at this convention in Finland in 2014 show how manga, anime, and cosplay are helping to spread Japanese values around the world.

violence. In other words, soft power relies on making a country appear more attractive to the target country. This can be achieved directly, such as through governments providing foreign aid, or indirectly, such as through the work of NGOs, education, and cultural exchange.

86 CD

35 **6** Think about different countries around the world and which ones you would like to visit. You probably would not want to visit a country which is dangerous or where the people are treated badly or have little freedom. Countries with stable democratic governments, which respect human rights, have reliable social institutions, such as police and health services, and which have strong economies are generally the most
40 attractive.

87 CD

7 Many countries have educational exchange programs, which allow students to spend time studying in a school in a different country. In addition, many countries also encourage students from other countries to study at their universities. This is a form of soft power because, in addition to the subjects studied, such students also learn about
45 the people, laws, politics, and culture of the country they are studying in. In this way, international students develop friendships with foreign people and come to appreciate their countries more.

88 CD

8 The aspect of soft power that we are probably most familiar with is culture. Many countries
50 showcase their traditional culture by encouraging tourists to visit historical places and experience unique cultural events. In addition, countries demonstrate their strength and ability by taking part in international sporting events such as the Olympic
55 Games. Finally, countries show us their ideals, values, and goals through popular media such as music, movies, anime, comics, computer games, and books. For example, Disney movies often present American values while Japanese values can be seen
60 in Studio Ghibli movies. Enjoying such cultural products can help us to understand other countries better and improve our opinion of them.

What messages about Japan do characters like Totoro send to the world?

89 CD

9 Soft power helps a country achieve change by encouraging other countries to

like them more. This may sound a little like advertising and this should not be
65　surprising. The goal of advertising is to create a good relationship between us and the
product, so that we buy the product. The goal of soft power is to create a good
relationship between countries so that one country can convince another to do what it
wants. However, advertising can sometimes fail, and so can soft power.

90 CD

10　One way that advertising can fail is if the product is not very good. For example,
70　very few people believe that North Korea is truly the "workers' paradise" that it
describes itself as. Such misleading government information is often called
propaganda. The US has also suffered from this problem. The US presents itself as a
supporter of democracy and human rights, but it has supported undemocratic,
oppressive countries and allowed torture, which is a crime against humanity. Actions
75　like these damaged the reputation of the US and greatly reduced its soft power.

91 CD

11　Learning about other countries and enjoying their culture is undoubtedly a good
thing. However, we should consider carefully whether another country is using its soft
power to change our views and why.

Notes

civil disobedience 「市民的不服従」非暴力的行為により政府などに抗議の意を示すこと。**NGO ＝ non-governmental organization** 「非政府組織」　**showcase** 「紹介する，披露する」　**propaganda** 「プロパガンダ」
政府などの主義・思想の宣伝。

🌐 Questions for Understanding

Part 1　Look at the following statements about the passage. Write T if the statement is True, and F if it is False. Write the number of the paragraph where you find the answer in the parenthesis.

1) _____ It is impossible to use soft power to change the government of your own country.　　　　　　　　　　　　　　　　　　　　　　　　[　]

2) _____ The goal of soft power is to achieve change without the use of violence.
　　　　　　　　　　　　　　　　　　　　　　　　　　　[　]

3) _____ Studying abroad helps us to learn about the values of another country.
　　　　　　　　　　　　　　　　　　　　　　　　　　　[　]

4) _____ Manga and anime are forms of soft power which spread Japanese values.
　　　　　　　　　　　　　　　　　　　　　　　　　　　[　]

Part 2 Look at the following questions about the passage. Check the best answer for each.

1. Which word has the closest meaning to the word "continuum" in Paragraph 2?

   a. ☐ cycle   b. ☐ scale   c. ☐ queue   d. ☐ opposite

2. Which of the following is **not** a form of soft power?

   a. ☐ A government providing foreign aid to another country

   b. ☐ A government encouraging tourists to visit famous places

   c. ☐ A government opposing human rights for its citizens

   d. ☐ A government sending a national team to the Olympic Games

3. What is propaganda?

   a. ☐ It is one country encouraging other countries to like them more.

   b. ☐ It is when a country creates an educational exchange program.

   c. ☐ It is when a country communicates incorrect information about itself.

   d. ☐ It is one country trying to convince another to do what it wants.

4. How did the US damage its reputation?

   a. ☐ By making low-quality Disney movies

   b. ☐ By taking part in the Olympic Games

   c. ☐ By supporting undemocratic countries

   d. ☐ By presenting itself as a "workers' paradise"

🌐 Summary   2-92 💿

Fill each space with the best word or phrase from the list below.

diplomacy	attitudes	convince	relies on	reputation	conflict

If you want to 1) _____ someone to do something for you, it is easier if you have a good relationship. The same is true of countries when they conduct international 2) _____. While hard power 3) _____ the use of actions such as war and other kinds of 4) _____, soft power focuses on developing a good 5) _____ with other countries. In this way, it becomes possible to slowly change the 6) _____ and behavior of people in another country.

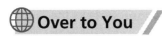 **Over to You**

Part 1 Ask and answer the following questions.

1. Have you ever been abroad?

2. What country would you most like to visit?

3. What country would you least like to visit?

4. Would you like to live in a different country?

5. What is one thing you would like to change about your country?

Part 2 Choose ONE of the statements below. Prepare a short response giving your opinion.

> • Countries should not try to change each other.
>
> • More foreign people should learn about my culture.

_____

_____

_____

_____

Part 3 Look at the statement below. Do you agree or disagree? Why? Share your opinion with your classmates and find out what they think.

> We should learn as much as we can about other countries.

Compiled References by Chapter

Many references were consulted in writing this book. The following is a list of the most useful, and we direct students and teachers who are interested in learning more about the issues raised in this book to them.

Culture and Society

Chapter 1   Who's the Fairest of Them All? – The Surprising Truth About Beauty

• BBC (2021, December 9). Saudi camel beauty pageant cracks down on cosmetic enhancements. *BBC News.* https://www.bbc.com/news/world-middle-east-59593001

• Brown, Z. & Tiggemann, M. (2016). Attractive celebrity and peer images on Instagram: Effect on women's mood and body image. *Body Image, 19*, 37-43. https://doi.org/10.1016/j.bodyim.2016.08.007

• Couture Bue, A.C. (2020). The looking glass selfie: Instagram use frequency predicts visual attention to high-anxiety body regions in young women. *Computers in Human Behavior, 108*, 106329. https://doi.org/10.1016/j.chb.2020.106329

• Donato, A. (n.d.). *Five of the Weirdest Animal Pageants Out There.* CBC. https://www.cbc.ca/cbcdocspov/features/five-of-the-weirdest-animal-pageants-out-there

• Faelens, L., Hoorelbeke, K., Cambier, R., van Put, J., Van de Putte, E., De Raedt, R. & Koster, E.H.W (2021). The relationship between Instagram use and indicators of mental health: A systematic review. *Computers in Human Behavior Reports, 4*, 100121. https://doi.org/10.1016/j.chbr.2021.100121

• Hönekopp, J. (2006). Once more: Is beauty in the eye of the beholder? Relative contributions of private and shared taste to judgments of facial attractiveness. *Journal of Experimental Psychology: Human Perception and Performance, 32*(2), 199–209. https://doi.org/ 10.1037/0096-1523.32.2.199

• Hosken, D.J. & House, C.M. (2011). Sexual Selection. *Current Biology, 21*(2), R62–R65. https://doi.org/ 10.1016/j.cub.2010.11.053

• Jamil, J. (2018, December 2). Viewpoint: Jameela Jamil on why airbrushing should be illegal. *BBC News.* https://www.bbc.com/news/world-46349307

• Lovejoy, B. (2016, February 22). *7 Unexpected Animal Beauty Pageants.* Mental Floss. https://www.mentalfloss.com/article/64567/7-unexpected-animal-beauty-pageants

• Ponkshe, A. & Endler, J. (2018). Effects of female preference intensity on the permissiveness of sexual trait polymorphisms. *Ecology and Evolution, 8*, 4518–4524. https://doi.org/10.1002/ece3.3957

• Sokolova, K., Kefi, H. & Dutot, V. (2022). Beyond the shallows of physical attractiveness: Perfection and objectifying gaze on Instagram. *International Journal of Information Management, 67*, 102546. https://doi.org/10.1016/j.ijinfomgt.2022.102546

• Wells, G., Horwitz, J. and Seetharaman, D. (2021). *Facebook knows Instagram is toxic for teen girls, company documents show.* Wall Street Journal. https://www.wsj.com/articles/facebook-knows-instagram-is-toxic-for-teen-girls-company-documents-show-11631620739

Chapter 2   Fan Fiction, Cosplay, and Rock Balancing – The World's Most Unusual Hobbies

• Ainley, N. (2016). Yes, balancing rocks is an art—If you're this good at it. *Vice.* https://www.vice.com/en/article/d749aj/stacking-rocks-balanced-art-master

• Attoun, M. (2007). Guinness World Record Feats. *American Profile.* https://americanprofile.com/articles/guiness-book-of-world-record-feats/

• Bernecker, K., & Becker, D. (2021). Beyond self-control: Mechanisms of hedonic goal pursuit and its relevance for well-being. *Personality and Social Psychology Bulletin, 47*(4), 627–642. https://doi.org/10.1177/0146167220941998

• Philippe, F.L., Vallerand, R.J. & Lavigne, G.L. (2009), Passion does make a difference in people's lives: A look at well-being in passionate and non-passionate individuals. *Applied Psychology: Health and Well-Being, 1*, 3-22. https://doi.org/10.1111/j.1758-0854.2008.01003.x

• Schellenberg, B. & Bailis, D. (2015). Can passion be polyamorous? The impact of having multiple passions on subjective well-being and momentary emotions. *Journal of Happiness Studies, 16*(6), 1365-1381. https://doi.org/10.1007/s10902-014-9564-x

- Wikipedia. (n.d). Button Collecting. *Wikipedia.* https://en.wikipedia.org/wiki/Button_collecting
- Wikipedia. (n.d). Comiket. *Wikipedia.* https://en.wikipedia.org/wiki/Comiket
- Wikipedia. (n.d). Cosplay. *Wikipedia.* https://en.wikipedia.org/wiki/Cosplay
- Wikipedia. (n.d). Dorodango. *Wikipedia.* https://en.wikipedia.org/wiki/Dorodango
- Wikipedia. (n.d). Fan Fiction. *Wikipedia.* https://en.wikipedia.org/wiki/Fan_fiction
- Wikipedia. (n.d). Fan Labor. *Wikipedia.* https://en.wikipedia.org/wiki/Fan_labor
- Wikipedia. (n.d). Rock Balancing. *Wikipedia.* https://en.wikipedia.org/wiki/Rock_balancing

Chapter 3   It's All a Part of the Game – The Ethics of Sports

- Malley, B. (2011). The 20 biggest scandals in sports history. *Bleacher Report.*
  https://bleacherreport.com/articles/854416-the-20-biggest-scandals-in-sports-history
- Seifert, K. (2020, January 18). What really happened during Deflategate? Five years later, the NFL's 'scandal' aged poorly. *ESPN.*
  https://www.espn.com/nfl/story/_/id/28502507/what-really-happened-deflategate-five-years-later-nfl-scandal-aged-poorly
- The Guardian (2018, November 30). 'Deeply shameful': 258 runners caught cheating in Shenzhen's half marathon: Fake race numbers, imposters and those cutting corners to face penalties, including lifetime bans. *The Guardian.*
  https://www.theguardian.com/world/2018/nov/30/deeply-shameful-258-runners-caught-cheating-in-shenzhens-half-marathon
- Vera, A. (2020, January 13). Before the Astros, 7 other cheating scandals that rocked the professional sports world. *CNN.*
  https://edition.cnn.com/2020/01/13/us/cheating-sports-scandals-trnd/index.html

Chapter 4   I'm Bored – How Boredom Can Be Good for Us

- Clear, J. (n.d.). How to fall in love with boredom and unlock your mental toughness.
  https://jamesclear.com/in-love-with-boredom
- Heshmat, S. (2020). 5 Benefits of boredom: How could we learn to benefit from boredom? *Psychology Today.*
  https://www.psychologytoday.com/us/blog/science-choice/202004/5-benefits-boredom
- Miller, G. (2022). The benefits of boredom: What kids can learn from handling more free time. *Child Mind Institute.*
  https://childmind.org/article/the-benefits-of-boredom/
- Robinson, B. (2020, September 2). Why neuroscientists say, 'Boredom is good for your brain's health. *Forbes.*
  https://www.forbes.com/sites/bryanrobinson/2020/09/02/why-neuroscientists-say-boredom-is-good-for-your-brains-health/?sh=5c9e27d71842
- Thomson, F. What is doomscrolling and why is it bad for us? *Open Access Government.*
  https://www.openaccessgovernment.org/what-is-doomscrolling-and-why-is-it-bad-for-us/143139/
- Walf, A. (2020). Let your brain rest: Boredom can be good for your health. *Rensselaer.*
  https://expertfile.com/spotlight/7393/let-your-brain-rest-boredom-can-be-good-for-your-health
- Wilson, T.D. Reinhard, D.A., Westgate, E.C., Gilbert, D.T., Ellerbeck, N., Hahn, C., Brown, C.L. & Shaked, A. (2014). Just think: The challenges of the disengaged mind. *Science, 345*(6192), pp. 75-77. https://doi.org/10.1126/science.1250830

Chapter 5   Go Whistle! – A Different Way of Communicating

- Holmes, B. (2021). Speaking in whistles: Dozens of traditional cultures use a whistled form of their native language for long-distance communication. You could, too. *Knowable Magazine.*
  https://knowablemagazine.org/article/mind/2021/whistled-languages
- Meyer, J. (2017, March 20). The Fascinating Art of Whistled Speech. *CNRS News.*
  https://news.cnrs.fr/opinions/the-fascinating-art-of-whistled-speech
- Robson, D. (2017, May 25). The beautiful languages of the people who talk like birds. *BBC.*
  https://www.bbc.com/future/article/20170525-the-people-who-speak-in-whistles

- Spinney, L. (2021, September 25). Could whistling shed light on the origins of speech? *The Guardian*. https://www.theguardian.com/science/2021/sep/25/could-whistling-shed-light-on-the-origins-of-speech-aas-shepherds-language
- Stein, E. (2017, July 31). Greece's disappearing whistled language. *BBC*. https://www.bbc.com/travel/article/20170731-greeces-disappearing-whistled-language
- Witzlack-Makarevich, A. and Nakagawa, H. (2019). 12 - Linguistic features and typologies in languages commonly referred to as 'Khoisan'. https://www.cambridge.org/core/books/abs/cambridge-handbook-of-african-linguistics/linguistic-features-and-typologies-in-languages-commonly-referred-to-as-khoisan/C867C6A27AA57A7E81366E5409D51302

Science and Technology

Chapter 6   Now You See It – What Magic Can Tell Us About Our Minds

- Frontiers in Psychology. (2016). *The psychology of magic and the magic of psychology*, Amir Raz, Jay A. Olson & Gustav Kuhn (eds.), Frontiers in Psychology.
- Kuhn, G. & Land, M.K. (2006). There's more to magic than meets the eye. *Current Biology*, *16*, R950-R951. https://doi.org/ 10.1016/j.cub.2006.10.012
- Sponner, W.E. & McEwan, G.F. (2007). Evidence for conjuring in Precolumbian Peru. *Andean Past*, *8*(14), 145-152. https://digitalcommons.library.umaine.edu/andean_past/vol8/iss1/14
- Wong. S. (2021, December 18). What doing magic tricks for birds is revealing about animal minds. *New Scientist*, *3365*.

Chapter 7   Creator or Created? – Social Media and Narcissism

- Bansal, A., Chandan, G., Abhijith, P. & Samiksha, G. (2018). Selfies: A boon or bane?, *Journal of Family Medicine and Primary Care*, *7*(4), 828–831. https://doi.org/10.4103/jfmpc.jfmpc_109_18
- Beyens, I., Pouwels, J.L., van Driel, I.I., Keijsers, L. & Valkenburg, P.M. (2020). The effect of social media on well-being differs from adolescent to adolescent. *Nature Scientific Reports*, *10*, 10763. https://doi.org/10.1038/s41598-020-67727-7
- Burnell, K. (2020). How narcissism relates to social media. *SPSP*. https://www.spsp.org/news-center/blog/burnell-narcissism-social-media
- Firestone, L. (2012). Is social media to blame for the rise in narcissism? https://www.psychalive.org/is-social-media-to-blame-for-the-rise-in-narcissism/
- Hayes, L. (2020). Social media is shaping a whole new generation of narcissists: Welcome to the 21st-century digital pandemic. *Medium*, *Mind Café*. https://medium.com/mind-cafe/social-media-is-shaping-a-whole-new-generation-of-narcissists-e3f6cd746131
- Reed, P. (2019). Narcissism and social media: Should we be afraid? *Psychology Today*. https://www.psychologytoday.com/us/blog/digital-world-real-world/201909/narcissism-and-social-media-should-we-be-afraid
- Newport Institute. (n.d.). Social media narcissism in young adults. *Newport Institute*. https://www.newportinstitute.com/resources/mental-health/social-media-narcissism/
- Sodha, S. (2021, November 7). Social media fuels narcissists' worst desires, making reasoned debate near impossible. *The Guardian*. https://www.theguardian.com/commentisfree/2021/nov/07/social-media-fuels-narcissists-worst-desires-making-reasoned-debate-near-impossible
- Twenge, J.L., Konrath, S., Foster, J.D., Campbell, W.K. & Bushman, B.J. (2008). Egos inflating over time: A cross-temporal meta-analysis of the Narcissistic Personality Inventory. *Journal of Personality*, *76*(4), 875-902. https://pubmed.ncbi.nlm.nih.gov/18507710/

Chapter 8   The Man With a Pig's Heart – What Is Xenotransplantation?

- BBC. (2022, March 9). Man given genetically modified pig heart dies. *BBC News*. https://www.bbc.com/news/

health-60681493
- CDC/National Center for Health Statistics (2022, September 6). Deaths and mortality. CDC. https://www.cdc.gov/nchs/fastats/deaths.htm
- Cengiz, N. & Wareham, C.S. (2020). Ethical considerations in xenotransplantation: A review. *Current Opinion in Organ Transplantation*, *25*(5), 483-488. https://doi.org/10.1097/MOT.0000000000000796
- Entwistle, J.W., Sade, R.M. & Drake, D.H. (2022). Clinical xenotransplantation seems close: Ethical issues persist. *Artificial Organs*, *46*(6), 987–994. https://doi.org/10.1111/aor.14255
- 日本臓器移植ネットワーク (n.d.). https://www.jotnw.or.jp/learn/about/
- Le Page, M. (2022, May 6). Man who received pig heart transplant has died after pig virus found. *New Scientist*, *3386.*

Chapter 9   Not Just a Flu Shot – How Vaccines Have Changed Our Lives

- Dubé, E., Laberge, C., Guay, M., Bramadat, P., Roy, R. & Bettinger, J.A. (2013). Vaccine hesitancy. *Human Vaccines & Immunotherapeutics*, *9*(8), 1763-1773. https://doi.org/10.4161/hv.24657
- Hornsey, M.J., Harris, E.A. & Fielding, K.S. (2018). The psychological roots of anti-vaccination attitudes: A 24-nation investigation. *Health Psychology*, *37*(4), 307-315.
- Hu, B., Huang, S. & Yin, L. (2021). The cytokine storm and COVID-19. *Journal of Medical Virology*, *93*(1), 250– 256. https://doi.org/10.1002/jmv.26232
- Jolley, D., Douglas, K.M. (2014). The effects of anti-vaccine conspiracy theories on vaccination intentions. *PLoS ONE*, *9*(2), e89177. https://doi.org/10.1371/journal.pone.0089177
- Kennedy, R.B., Ovsyannikova, I. & Poland, G.A. (2009). Smallpox vaccines for biodefense. *Vaccine*, *27*(4), D73-D79. https://doi.org/10.1016/j.vaccine.2009.07.103.
- Klein, A. (2022, June 22). Personalised cancer vaccines are finally beating hard to treat tumours. *New Scientist*, *3392.*
- Lei, J., Ploner, A., Elfström, K.M., Wang, J., Roth, R., Fang, F., Sundström, K., Dillner, J., & Sparén, P. (2020). HPV vaccination and the risk of invasive cervical cancer. *New England Journal of Medicine*, *383*, 1340-1348. https://doi.org/10.1056/NEJMoa1917338
- McNeil, M.M., Gee, J., Weintraub, E.S., Belongia, E.A., Lee, G.M., Glanz, J.M., Nordin, J.D., Klein, N.P., Baxter, R., Naleway, A.L., Jackson, L.A., Omer, S.B., Jacobsen, S.J. & DeStefano, F. (2014). The Vaccine Safety Datalink: Successes and challenges monitoring vaccine safety. *Vaccine*, *32*(42), 5390-5398. https://doi.org/10.1016/j.vaccine.2014.07.073.
- Murphy, J., Vallières, F., Bentall, R.P., Shevlin, M., McBride, O., Hartman, T.K., McKay, R., Bennett, K., Mason, L., Gibson-Miller, J., Levita, L., Martinez, A.P., Stocks, T.V.A., Karatzias, T. & Hyland, P. (2021). Psychological characteristics associated with COVID-19 vaccine hesitancy and resistance in Ireland and the United Kingdom. Nature Communications, 12, 29. https://doi.org/10.1038/s41467-020-20226-9
- Reyes, R., Ahn, R., Thurber, K., Burke, T.F. (2013). Urbanization and infectious diseases: General principles, historical perspectives, and contemporary challenges. In: Fong, I. (eds) *Challenges in infectious diseases. Emerging infectious diseases of the 21st century*. Springer: New York. https://doi.org/10.1007/978-1-4614-4496-1_4
- Rota, P.A., Moss, W.J., Takeda, M., de Swart, R.L., Thompson K.M. & Goodson, J.L. (2016). Measles. *Nature Reviews. Disease Primers, 2*, 16049. https://doi.org/10.1038/nrdp.2016.49
- Simms, K.T., Hanley, S.J.B., Smith, M.A., Keane, A. & Canfell, K. (2020). Impact of HPV vaccine hesitancy on cervical cancer in Japan: a modelling study. *The Lancet Public Health*, *5*(4), 223-234. https://doi.org/10.1016/S2468-2667(20)30010-4
- Wharton, M. (2010). Vaccine safety: Current systems and recent findings. *Current Opinion in Pediatrics*, *22*(1), 88-93. https://doi.org/10.1097/MOP.0b013e3283350425
- Yagi, A., Ueda, Y., Ikeda, S., Miyagi, E., Sekine, M., Enomoto, T. & Kimura, T. (2022). The looming health hazard: A wave of HPV-related cancers in Japan is becoming a reality due to the continued suspension of the governmental recommendation of HPV vaccine. *The Lancet Regional Health Western Pacific, 18,* 100327. https://doi.org/10.1016/j.lanwpc.2021.100327

Chapter 10   Bad Air – The Hidden Dangers of Air Pollution
- Bartington, S. and Avis, W. (2020). *Prevalence of health impacts related to exposure to poor air quality among children in Low and Lower Middle-Income Countries*. Knowledge, evidence and learning for development. https://opendocs.ids.ac.uk/opendocs/bitstream/handle/20.500.12413/15689/775_Health_impacts_of_air_polllution_in_LICs_and_LMICs.pdf?sequence=1&isAllowed=y
- Mackenzie, J. and Turrentine, J. (2021). Air pollution: Everything you need to know: How smog, soot, greenhouse gases, and other top air pollutants are affecting the planet—and your health. *NRDC*. https://www.nrdc.org/stories/air-pollution-everything-you-need-know
- McMurray, C. (2004). *Current smoking trends in U.S., Canada, Britain. Gallup.* https://news.gallup.com/poll/10762/current-smoking-trends-us-canada-britain.aspx
- Mingzhao, L. (2021). *5 dangerous pollutants you're breathing in every day. United Nations Environment Program.* https://www.unep.org/news-and-stories/story/5-dangerous-pollutants-youre-breathing-every-day
- Mui, S. & Levin, A. (2020). *Clearing the air: The benefits of the clean air act. NRDC.* https://www.nrdc.org/resources/clean-air-acts-benefits-map
- Rutledge, K. *et al.* (2022). Air pollution. *National Geographic.* https://education.nationalgeographic.org/resource/air-pollution
- Smoke Free World. (2022). State of smoking in the United Kingdom. *Smoke Free World.* https://www.smokefreeworld.org/health-science-research-2/health-science-technology-agenda/data-analytics/global-state-of-smoking-landscape/state-smoking-united-kingdom/
- State of Global Air. (2022). The latest data on air quality and health where you live and around the globe. *State of Global Air.* https://www.stateofglobalair.org/
- World Health Organization. (2022). Air pollution. *WHO.* https://www.who.int/health-topics/air-pollution
- World Health Organization. (2022). Billions of people still breathe unhealthy air: new WHO data: Over 6000 cities now monitor air quality. *WHO.* https://www.who.int/news/item/04-04-2022-billions-of-people-still-breathe-unhealthy-air-new-who-data
- World Health Organization. (2023). Clean household energy solutions toolkit (CHEST). *WHO.* https://www.who.int/tools/clean-household-energy-solutions-toolkit
- World Health Organization. (2022). How air pollution is destroying our health. *WHO.* https://www.who.int/news-room/spotlight/how-air-pollution-is-destroying-our-health#:~:text=They%20can%20increase%20the%20risk,inflammation%20and%20reduced%20lung%20function

Business and Economics
Chapter 11   Marketing Mistakes – When Advertising Doesn't Pay
- Bowerman, M. (2015). McDonald's pulls ad that 'exploited child bereavement'. *USA Today.* https://www.usatoday.com/story/news/nation-now/2015/11/12/bloomingdales-sorry-inappropriate-spiked-eggnog-ad/75646374/
- Doctor, D. (2017). Audi faces backlash for sexist ad. *AdNews.* https://www.adnews.com.au/news/audi-faces-backlash-for-sexist-ad
- Eisenstein, P.A. (2013). Ford apologizes for ads showing bound, gagged women. *NBC News.* https://www.nbcnews.com/business/business-news/ford-apologizes-ads-showing-bound-gagged-women-flna1b9046338
- Lalley, M. (2023). 20 of the biggest marketing fails of all time (and why they sucked). *Business2Community.* https://www.business2community.com/marketing/20-of-the-biggest-marketing-fails-of-all-time-and-why-they-sucked-02287809
- Siddique, H. (2017). McDonald's pulls ad that 'exploited child bereavement'. *The Guardian.* https://www.theguardian.com/business/2017/may/16/mcdonalds-apologises-over-ad-exploiting-child-bereavement
- Slawson, N. (2017). Dove apologises for ad showing black woman turning into white one. *The Guardian.* https://www.theguardian.com/world/2017/oct/08/dove-apologises-for-ad-showing-black-woman-turning-into-

white-one
- Sony PlayStation – White is coming billboard.
  https://criticalmediaproject.org/sony-playstation-white-is-coming-billboard-2/
- The 8 biggest marketing fail of all time (with practical takeaways). (2021). *WordStream*.
  https://www.wordstream.com/blog/ws/2021/12/28/marketing-fails
- Wang, A.B. (2017). Nivea's 'White Is Purity' ad campaign didn't end well. *The Washington Post*.
  https://www.washingtonpost.com/news/business/wp/2017/04/05/niveas-white-is-purity-ad-campaign-didnt-end-well/

Chapter 12   Bought and Sold – Who Owns Life?

- Coppock, A., Hill, S.J. & Vavreck, L. (2020). The small effects of political advertising are small regardless of context, message, sender, or receiver: Evidence from 59 real-time randomized experiments. *Science Advances*, 6(36), eabc4046. https://doi.org/ 10.1126/sciadv.abc4046
- Fowler, E.F., Franz, M.M., Martin, G.J., Peskowitz, Z. & Ridout, T.N. (2021). Political advertising online and offline. *American Political Science Review*, *115*(1), 130-149.
  https://doi.org/10.1017/S0003055420000696
- Groos, D. & van Veen, E.B. (2020). Anonymised data and the rule of law. *European Data Protection Law Review*, *498*. https://heinonline.org/HOL/LandingPage?handle=hein.journals/edpl6&div=72&id=&page=Anonymised Data and the Rule of Law
- Haenschen, K. & Jennings, J. (2019). Mobilizing Millennial voters with targeted internet advertisements: A field experiment, *Political Communication*, *36*(3), 357-375. https://doi.org/10.1080/10584609.2018.1548530
- Hager, H. (2019). Do online ads influence vote choice? *Political Communication*, *36*(3), 376-393. https://doi.org/ 10.1080/10584609.2018.1548529
- Huq, A.Z. (2021, October 25). Who owns our data? *Boston Review*. https://www.bostonreview.net/articles/who-owns-our-data/
- Jurcys, P., Donewald, C., Fenwick, M., Lampinen, M., Nekrošius, V. & Smaliukas, A. (2021). Ownership of user-held data: Why property law is the right approach. *Harvard Journal of Law & Technology Digest*. https://jolt.law.harvard.edu/digest/ownership-of-user-held-data-why-property-law-is-the-right-approach
- Kreiss, D. & Mcgregor, S.C. (2019). The "Arbiters of What Our Voters See": Facebook and Google's struggle with policy, process, and enforcement around political advertising, *Political Communication*, *36*(4), 499-522. https://doi.org/10.1080/10584609.2019.1619639
- Lawton, G. (2023, February 8). The push to grant legal rights to nature is gaining momentum. *New Scientist*, *3425*.
- Ni, C., Cang, L.S., Gope, P. & Min, G. (2022). Data anonymization evaluation for big data and IoT environment. *Information Sciences*, *605*, 381-392. https://doi.org/10.1016/j.ins.2022.05.040.
- Thouvenin, F. & Tamò-Larrieux, A. (2021). Data ownership and data access rights – Meaningful tools for promoting the European digital single market? In: Burri, M. (ed) *Big Data and Global Trade Law*. Cambridge University Press: Cambridge. https://www.cambridge.org/core/books/big-data-and-global-trade-law/data-ownership-and-data-access-rights/BC314C63C58A09C4B9C5D55894FE68C6
- Wikipedia. (n.d). Alder Hey Organs Scandal. *Wikipedia*. https://en.wikipedia.org/wiki/Alder_Hey_organs_scandal
- Wikipedia. (n.d). Biological Patent. *Wikipedia*. https://en.wikipedia.org/wiki/Biological_patent
- Wikipedia. (n.d). Henrietta Lacks. *Wikipedia*. https://en.wikipedia.org/wiki/Henrietta_Lacks
- World Bank. (2021). Who owns personal data? *World Development Report 2021*. https://wdr2021.worldbank.org/spotlights/who-owns-personal-data/

Chapter 13   The High Price of Poverty – What Is the Poverty Premium?

- Chetty, R., Stepner, M., Abraham, S., Lin, S., Scuderi, B., Turner, N., Bergeron, A. & Cutler, D. (2016). The association between income and life expectancy in the United States, 2001-2014. *Journal of the American Medical Association*, *315*(16), 1750-66. https://doi.org/10.1001/jama.2016.4226
  CSRI. (2022). *Global Wealth Report, 2022*. Zürich: Credit Suisse Research Institute.

- Goal 1. (n.d.). End poverty in all its forms everywhere. *United Nations Sustainable Development Goals*. https://sdgs.un.org/goals/goal1
- Inequality.org (n.d.). Global inequality. *Inequality.org*. https://inequality.org/facts/global-inequality/
- Milanovic, B. (2016). *Global inequality: A new approach for the age of globalization*. Cambridge, MA: Belknap Press.
- Piketty, T. (2014). *Capital in the twenty-first century*. Cambridge, MA: Harvard University Press.
- Wikipedia. (n.d). Distribution of wealth. *Wikipedia*. https://en.wikipedia.org/wiki/Distribution_of_wealth
- Wikipedia. (n.d). Extreme poverty. *Wikipedia*. https://en.wikipedia.org/wiki/Extreme_poverty
- Wikipedia. (n.d). Poverty. *Wikipedia*. https://en.wikipedia.org/wiki/Poverty
- Stiglitz, J. (2012). *The price of inequality: How today's divided society endangers our future*. New York: W.W. Norton, 2012.

Chapter 14   Every Little Helps – How Much Money Do We Need?

- Gössling, S., Kees, J. & Litman, T. (2022). The lifetime cost of driving a car. *Ecological Economics*, 194, 107335. https://doi.org/10.1016/j.ecolecon.2021.107335
- japanguide.com (n.d.). Living costs. *japanguide.com*. https://www.japan-guide.com/e/e2202.html
- Ministry of Health, Labor and Welfare. (2017). *Comprehensive Survey of Living Conditions 2015*. Tokyo: Ministry of Health, Labor and Welfare.
- Martin, A.K.T. (2022, October 17). Work forever: Japan's seniors brace for life without retirement. *The Japan Times*. https://www.japantimes.co.jp/news/2022/10/17/business/senior-employment-japan/
- The Japan Times. (2019, June 18). Another Japanese government estimate indicates up to ¥30 million in savings needed per couple after retirement. *The Japan Times*. https://www.japantimes.co.jp/news/2019/06/18/business/another-japanese-government-estimate-indicates-%C2%A530-million-savings-needed-per-couple-retirement/
- The Japan Times. (2001, May 15). Raising child costs 63 million yen: study. *The Japan Times*. https://www.japantimes.co.jp/news/2001/05/15/national/raising-child-costs-63-million-yen-study/
- The Nippon Foundation (n.d.). Addressing child poverty. *The Nippon Foundation*. https://www.nippon-foundation.or.jp/en/what/projects/ending_child_poverty
- Webb, W.S. (2023, February 20). Good financial advice hasn't changed in 300 years. *The Japan Times*. https://www.japantimes.co.jp/opinion/2023/02/20/commentary/world-commentary/investing-history/

Chapter 15   The Cost of Learning – What Is Education Worth?

- Coursera. (2022). Is a bachelor's degree worth it? *Coursera*.
  https://www.coursera.org/articles/is-a-bachelors-degree-worth-it
- Franklin University. (2022). Is a bachelor's degree worth it? Sorting fact from fiction. *Franklin University*.
  https://www.franklin.edu/blog/is-a-bachelors-degree-worth-it
- Lowe, R.J. (2015). Cram schools in Japan: The need for research. *The Language Teacher*, *31*(9), 26-31.
  https://jalt-publications.org/sites/default/files/pdf-article/39.1tlt_art5.pdf
- Nippon.com. (2019, August 26). Cost of education soars in Japan while wages stand still. *Nippon.com*.
  https://www.nippon.com/en/japan-data/h00522/cost-of-education-soars-in-japan-while-wages-stand-still.html#:~:text=A%20survey%20on%20the%20current,%2C%20clothes%2C%20and%20other%20items.
- Semuels, A. (2017). Japan might be what equality in education looks like. *The Atlantic*.
  https://www.theatlantic.com/business/archive/2017/08/japan-equal-education-school-cost/535611/
- Statista. (2022). Enrollment rate in school education in Japan in school year 2020, by institution type. *Statista*.
  https://www.statista.com/statistics/1189581/japan-attendance-rate-students-by-type-of-institution/#:~:text=Qualities%20of%20the%20Japanese%20educational,in%20all%20rounds%20of%20assessment.
- Tretina, K. & Hahn, A. (2022). Is college worth the cost? Pros vs cons. *Forbes*.
  https://www.forbes.com/advisor/student-loans/is-college-worth-it/#:~:text=Despite%20the%20rising%20cost%20of,only%20a%20high%20school%20diploma

Politics and International Relations

Chapter 16   Help or Hindrance? – The Impact of Foreign Aid

- Development Aid. (2017). Pros and cons of humanitarian aid. *Development Aid.*
  https://www.developmentaid.org/news-stream/post/80/80-2
- Ilasco, I. (2020). Foreign aid and top donor countries in 2020. *Development Aid.*
  https://www.developmentaid.org/news-stream/post/92614/foreign-aid-and-top-donor-countries-in-2020
- Kenton, W. (2021). What is foreign aid? Forms of aid, statistics, and examples. *Investopedia.*
  https://www.investopedia.com/terms/f/foreign-aid.asp
- Regoli, N. (2019). *20 advantages and disadvantages of foreign aid to developing countries. Connect Us.*
  https://connectusfund.org/20-advantages-and-disadvantages-of-foreign-aid-to-developing-countries
- Williams, V. (2022). Foreign Aid. *Britannica.*
  https://www.britannica.com/topic/foreign-aid

Chapter 17   How to Change the World – Peaceful Protest

- Coates Ulrichsen, K. (2013). Bahrain's uprising: Regional dimensions and international consequences. *Stability Journal.*
  https://stabilityjournal.org/articles/10.5334/sta.be
- De Guzman, C. (2023). The Philippines once celebrated Marcos' fall. Under his son, has the country moved on? *Time.*
  https://time.com/6257017/philippines-bongbong-marcos-people-power-revolution/
- Kandelaki, G. (2006). Georgia's Rose Revolution: A participant's perspective. *United States Institute of Peace.*
  https://www.usip.org/sites/default/files/sr167.pdf
- Klein, A. (2019, October 16). These evidence-based strategies may turn the tide on domestic violence. *New Scientist.*
  https://www.newscientist.com/article/mg24432524-800-these-evidence-based-strategies-may-turn-the-tide-on-domestic-violence/
- Marks, Z., Chenoweth, E. & Okeke, J. (2019). People power is rising in Africa: How protest movements are succeeding where even global arrest warrants can't. *Foreign Affairs.*
  https://www.foreignaffairs.com/articles/africa/2019-04-25/people-power-rising-africa
- Robson, D. (2019, May 13). Nonviolent protests are twice as likely to succeed as armed conflicts – and those engaging a threshold of 3.5% of the population have never failed to bring about change. *BBC.*
  https://www.bbc.com/future/article/20190513-it-only-takes-35-of-people-to-change-the-world
- Stephan, M.J. & Chenoweth, E. (2008). Why civil resistance works: The strategic logic of nonviolent conflict. *International Security, 33*(1), 7–44.
  https://www.belfercenter.org/sites/default/files/legacy/files/IS3301_pp007-044_Stephan_Chenoweth.pdf

Chapter 18   It's My Right – How Do We Balance Competing Rights?

- Committee on Bioethics (1997). Religious objections to medical care. Pediatrics, 99(2), 279–281. https://doi.org/10.1542/peds.99.2.279
- Elkins, Z. & Ginsburg, T. (2022). Imagining a world without the Universal Declaration of Human Rights. *World Politics, 74*(3), 327–366. https://doi.org/10.1017/S0043887122000065
- Newell, P. (1993). The child's right to physical integrity. The International Journal of Children's Rights. 1, 101–104. https://doi.org/10.1163/157181893X00368
- Rodham, H (1973). Children under the law. *Harvard Educational Review, 43*(4), 487–514. https://doi.org/10.17763/haer.43.4.e14676283875773k
- Steiner, H.J. & Philip Alston, P. (2000). *International human rights in context: Law, politics, morals,* (2nd ed). Oxford: Oxford University Press.
- Tomuschat, C. (2016). Protection of human rights under universal international law. *UN Chronicle, 53*(4). https://www.un.org/en/chronicle/article/protection-human-rights-under-universal-international-law
- Wikipedia. (n.d). Human rights. *Wikipedia.*
  https://en.wikipedia.org/wiki/Human_rights

- Wikipedia. (n.d). International bill of human rights. *Wikipedia.*
  https://en.wikipedia.org/wiki/International_Bill_of_Human_Rights
- Wikipedia. (n.d). Universal declaration of human rights. *Wikipedia.*
  https://en.wikipedia.org/wiki/Universal_Declaration_of_Human_Rights

Chapter 19   Population Power – The Economic Impact of Immigration

- Bannerman, L. (2022). Farm worker shortage brings a bitter harvest. *The Times.*
  https://www.thetimes.co.uk/article/farm-worker-shortage-brings-a-bitter-harvest-stjmpdn5q
- Dustmann, C., Frattini, T. & Preston, I.P. (2013). The effect of immigration along the distribution of wages.
  Review of Economic Studies, *80*, 145–173.
  https://www.ucl.ac.uk/~uctpb21/Cpapers/Review%20of%20Economic%20Studies-2013-Dustmann-145-73.
  pdf
- Migration Advisory Committee. (2018). EEA migration in the UK: Final report. *Migration Advisory Committee.*
  https://assets.publishing.service.gov.uk/government/uploads/system/uploads/attachment_data/file/741926/
  Final_EEA_report.PDF
- ESRC. (2022). Immigration and the UK labour market: The latest evidence from economic research. *ESRC, The
  London School of Economics and Political Science.*
  https://cep.lse.ac.uk/pubs/download/pa014.pdf
- Natarajan, A., Moslimani, M. andLopez, M.H. (2022). Key facts about recent trends in global migration. *Pew
  Research Center.*
  https://www.pewresearch.org/fact-tank/2022/12/16/key-facts-about-recent-trends-in-global-
  migration/#:~:text=The%20number%20of%20international%20migrants,Organization%20for%20
  Migration%20(IOM).
- Pettinger, T. (2022). Pros and cons of immigration. *Economics Help.*
  https://www.economicshelp.org/blog/152453/economics/pros-and-cons-of-immigration/
- Vargas-Silva, C. (2022). The labour market effects of immigration. *The Migration Observatory.*
  https://migrationobservatory.ox.ac.uk/resources/briefings/the-labour-market-effects-of-immigration/
- IOM. (2022). World migration report 2022. *IOM, UN Migration.*
  https://worldmigrationreport.iom.int/wmr-2022-interactive/

Chapter 20   Anime, Disney, and Democracy – What Is Soft Power?

- Afoaku, Osita G. (2000). U.S. foreign policy and authoritarian regimes: Change and continuity in international
  clientelism. *Journal of Third World Studies*, *17*(2), 13–40. *JSTOR 45198191*
- Brassett, J. (2016). British comedy, global resistance: Russell Brand, Charlie Brooker and Stewart Lee. *European
  Journal of International Relations*, *22*(1), 168–191. https://doi.org/10.1177/1354066115586816
- Harbury, J. (2005), *Truth, torture, and the American Way: The history and consequences of U.S. involvement in
  torture.* Boston: Beacon Press.
- Nye, J.S. (2021): Soft power: the evolution of a concept. *Journal of Political Power*, *14*(1), 196-208. https://doi.
  org/10.1080/2158379X.2021.1879572
- Rothman, S.B. (2011) Revising the soft power concept: what are the means and mechanisms of soft power?
  Journal of Political Power, *4*(1), 49-64, https://doi.org/10.1080/2158379X.2011.556346
- Solomon, T. (2014) The affective underpinnings of soft power. *European
  Journal of International Relations*, *20*(3), 720-741. https://doi.org/10.1177/1354066113503479
- Wojciuk, A., Michałek, M. & Stormowska, M. (2015). Education as a source and tool of soft power in
  international relations. *European Political Science 14*, 298–317. https://doi.org/10.1057/eps.2015.25
- Wikipedia. (n.d). Sayyid Qutb. *Wikipedia.* https://en.wikipedia.org/wiki/Sayyid_Qutb
- Zamorano, M.M. (2016). Reframing cultural diplomacy: The instrumentalization of culture under the soft power
  theory. *Journal of Current Cultural Research*, *8*(2): open articles. https://doi.org/10.3384/
  cu.2000.1525.1608165

TEXT PRODUCTION STAFF

edited by	編集
Minako Hagiwara	萩原 美奈子

cover design by	表紙デザイン
Nobuyoshi Fujino	藤野 伸芳

CD PRODUCTION STAFF

narrated by	吹き込み者
Howard Colefield　(AmE)	ハワード・コルフィールド（アメリカ英語）
Jennifer Okano　(AmE)	ジェニファー・オカノ（アメリカ英語）

Grand Tour – New Discoveries
新たな時代への冒険

2024年1月10日　初版印刷
2024年1月20日　初版発行

著　　者	Anthony Sellick
	James Bury
	堀内 香織
発 行 者	佐野 英一郎
発 行 所	株式会社 成 美 堂
	〒101-0052　東京都千代田区神田小川町3-22
	TEL 03-3291-2261　FAX 03-3293-5490
	https://www.seibido.co.jp

印 刷・製 本　萩原印刷株式会社

ISBN 978-4-7919-7293-7　　　　　　　　Printed in Japan